Martin D. Caldwell

Archangels of Neoplatonism
Emanation of the Sacred

Original Title: *Archangels of Neoplatonism – Emanation of the Sacred*

Copyright © 2024, published by Luiz Antonio dos Santos ME. This book is a non-fiction work that explores Neoplatonism and its spiritual archetypes. Through a philosophical and metaphysical approach, the author presents a profound study of the relationship between the divine and the manifest world, the structures of reality, and the path of return to primordial unity.

1st Edition
Production Team
Author: Martin D. Caldwell
Editor: Luiz Santos
Cover Design: Studios Booklas / Alexander Vieri
Consultant: Edgar Monteiro
Researchers: Helena Vasconcelos, Thomas Ferrer, Sofia Albuquerque
Typesetting: Ricardo Menezes
Translation: Victor Hargreaves
Publication and Identification
Archangels of Neoplatonism – Emanation of the Sacred
Booklas, 2024
Categories: Philosophy / Metaphysics / Spirituality
DDC: 186 (Neoplatonism) – **CDU:** 1(091)

All rights reserved to:
Luiz Antonio dos Santos ME / Booklas Publishing
No part of this book may be reproduced, stored in a retrieval system, or transmitted by any means—electronic, mechanical, photocopying, recording, or otherwise—without prior and express permission from the copyright holder.

Summary

Sistematic Index 5
Prologue 11
Chapter 1 The Philosophical Context of Neoplatonism............... 13
Chapter 2 Neoplatonic Thought 18
Chapter 3 The Concept of Hypostases 25
Chapter 4 Divine Reality.. 31
Chapter 5 Absolute Transcendence... 37
Chapter 6 The Emanation of Divine Thought............................. 42
Chapter 7 The Connection with the Sensible World................... 47
Chapter 8 One, Intellect, and Soul 53
Chapter 9 The Dynamics of Emanation...................................... 59
Chapter 10 The Cosmic Order and the Hypostases 65
Chapter 11 Primary Hypostases.. 72
Chapter 12 The Legacy of the Hypostases.................................. 78
Chapter 13 Aeons, the Intermediate Beings................................ 84
Chapter 14 Divine Plenitude 89
Chapter 15 Time and Eternity 95
Chapter 16 Divine Qualities... 100
Chapter 17 Aeons and Archangels.. 106
Chapter 18 The Philosophy of Plotinus 113
Chapter 19 Other Neoplatonists 119
Chapter 20 The Ascent of the Soul 126
Chapter 21 Invocation of the Aeons 132

Chapter 22 Critiques and Challenges to the Understanding of Aeons 138
Chapter 23 Mythical and Poetic Imagination 144
Chapter 24 Archetypes of Human Experience 150
Chapter 25 Contemporary Spirituality 156
Chapter 26 Personal Applications 162
Chapter 27 The Meaning of Life 168
Chapter 28 Harmony with the Divine Order 175
Chapter 29 Directions for Future Investigations 182
Chapter 30 Towards the Divine 188
Epilogue 194
Glossary of Neoplatonic Terms 196

Sistematic Index

Chapter 1: The Philosophical Context of Neoplatonism - Situates Neoplatonism within its historical context, exploring the social, political, and intellectual conditions that fostered its flourishing.

Chapter 2: Neoplatonic Thought - Explores the key concepts that form the basis of Neoplatonic thought, including reality as emanation from the One, divine transcendence and immanence, and the importance of contemplation and the ascetic journey.

Chapter 3: The Concept of Hypostases - Delves into the concept of hypostases, the levels of divine reality that emanate from the One, and their significance in Neoplatonic cosmology, metaphysics, and soteriology.

Chapter 4: Divine Reality - Explores the Neoplatonic understanding of divine reality, characterized by its transcendence, immanence, ineffability, and the distinction between the transcendent divine and the manifest divine.

Chapter 5: Absolute Transcendence - Focuses on the One, the first hypostasis and source of all reality, emphasizing its ineffability, unknowability, and its role as the primordial principle from which everything emanates.

Chapter 6: The Emanation of Divine Thought - Discusses the Intellect (Nous), the second hypostasis, which emerges as the first emanation of the One, and its role as the domain of divine thought, the realm of Platonic Forms, and the seat of cosmic intelligence.

Chapter 7: The Connection with the Sensible World - Explores the Soul (Psyché), the third primary hypostasis, which acts as a bridge between the intelligible world and the sensible world, animating and organizing the cosmos.

Chapter 8: One, Intellect, and Soul - Compares and contrasts the characteristics and attributes of the three primary hypostases, revealing the progressive differentiation and complexification of reality as it emanates from its primordial source.

Chapter 9: The Dynamics of Emanation - Examines the dynamic of procession (proodos) and conversion (epistrophe), the essential movement of reality from the One towards multiplicity and the return of all creation to its primordial origin.

Chapter 10: The Cosmic Order and the Hypostases - Explores how the hypostases manifest in the cosmic order, revealing the Neoplatonic vision of the universe as a living and hierarchical organism, and the position of the human being within this cosmic structure.

Chapter 11: Primary Hypostases - Discusses the interpretations and variations in the understanding of the primary hypostases among the main Neoplatonists, including Plotinus, Porphyry, Proclus, and Iamblichus.

Chapter 12: The Legacy of the Hypostases - Traces the influence of the primary hypostases on Western philosophy and thought, from medieval and Renaissance philosophy to mysticism, theology, and contemporary resonances.

Chapter 13: Aeons, the Intermediate Beings - Introduces the concept of Aeons, intermediate beings that emanate from the Intellect or the Soul, and their function as mediators between the primary hypostases and the manifest world.

Chapter 14: Divine Plenitude - Explores the Pleroma, the transcendent realm of the Aeons, and its hierarchical structure, revealing the relationships of interdependence and emanation that connect the Aeons.

Chapter 15: Time and Eternity - Examines the relationship between the Aeons and the notions of time and eternity, exploring their temporal and atemporal nature and how they influence our perception of time in the material world.

Chapter 16: Divine Qualities - Discusses how the Aeons personify divine qualities within the Pleroma, revealing the variety and richness of these qualities and how the contemplation of the Aeons can lead to communion with these virtues.

Chapter 17: Aeons and Archangels - Compares and contrasts Aeons and Archangels, two categories of intermediary beings, identifying their parallels and distinctions in terms of mediating functions, hierarchical position, and connection with the divine.

Chapter 18: The Philosophy of Plotinus - Explores Plotinus' implicit vision of Aeons, where the emphasis falls on the richness and diversity of the Divine Intelligence itself, rather than on a rigid hierarchy of separate entities.

Chapter 19: Other Neoplatonists - Discusses how Iamblichus and Proclus, successors of Plotinus, expanded and systematized the concept of Aeons, transforming them into central elements of late Neoplatonic cosmology.

Chapter 20: The Ascent of the Soul - Examines how the Aeons manifest as essential steps and guides in the soul's journey towards mystical union with the Divine, revealing the progressive and hierarchical nature of the Neoplatonic spiritual path.

Chapter 21: Invocation of the Aeons - Explores practical methods for establishing a conscious connection with the Aeons, including guided meditation, creative visualization, mantras, chants, contemplative prayer, and formal invocation.

Chapter 22: Critiques and Challenges to the Understanding of Aeons - Analyzes the difficulties and challenges in understanding the concept of Aeons, addressing criticisms and objections of a philosophical, theological, and contemporary nature.

Chapter 23: Mythical and Poetic Imagination - Explores the relationship between Aeons and mythical and poetic imagination, revealing a more intuitive and experiential dimension of spiritual knowledge, where beauty, emotion, and imagination become paths to understanding the Divine.

Chapter 24: Archetypes of Human Experience - Investigates the Aeons as archetypes of human experience, revealing their connection to universal and primordial patterns of the human psyche and their relevance to self-knowledge and the realization of human potential.

Chapter 25: Contemporary Spirituality - Discusses the contemporary relevance of Neoplatonism and hypostases, demonstrating their practical and transformative value for the spiritual and existential quest of modern human beings.

Chapter 26: Personal Applications - Explores the practical applications of Neoplatonic principles and the knowledge of hypostases in daily life, including contemplative reflection, cultivation of virtue, meditation, interpersonal relationships, appreciation of beauty, and the search for meaning.

Chapter 27: The Meaning of Life - Examines the Neoplatonic perspective on the meaning of life, proposing a path to understanding our place in the universe and our soul's journey towards returning to its primordial origin, the One.

Chapter 28: Harmony with the Divine Order - Discusses Neoplatonic ethics, which is intrinsically linked to metaphysics, where the pursuit of virtue and moral conduct are essential paths for the soul's ascension and union with the Divine.

Chapter 29: Directions for Future Investigations - Outlines areas of open questions and future research in Neoplatonism, including the interpretation of concepts, historical contextualization, comparative approaches, contemporary relevance, and methodological approaches.

Chapter 30: Towards the Divine - Reflects on the intrinsic importance of studying Neoplatonism and the hypostases, emphasizing its lasting value for self-knowledge, spiritual growth, and the search for meaning, purpose, and connection with the transcendent.

Chapter 31: Glossary of Neoplatonic Terms - Provides concise and accessible definitions of the most important Neoplatonic terms, demystifying the vocabulary and facilitating the understanding of key concepts.

Prologue

There is a knowledge that is not limited to the intellect, but resonates in the soul. A knowledge that not only describes reality, but reveals its invisible structures and fundamental principles. Throughout the centuries, seekers of truth have tried to understand the hidden order of the cosmos, guided by the certainty that the universe is not an arbitrary chaos, but an emanation of a supreme principle.

The Neoplatonic tradition, presented here with philosophical rigor and contemplative depth, offers a map of this reality. More than a system of thought, it is a path that leads from the multiple to the one, from sensible dispersion to intelligible unity, from the fragmentation of the material world to the perfection of the divine intellect. The hypostases — the One, Intellect, and Soul — structure this vision, unfolding in hierarchical orders that link the human to the transcendent.

As the reader progresses through these pages, they will encounter concepts that have underpinned both Western metaphysics and the mystical traditions inspired by it. Here, the relationships between divine reality and the manifest world, the celestial intermediaries that guide the soul on its journey of return, and the nature of knowledge that transcends discursive thought are explored.

This book does not demand faith, but a willingness to understand. It does not impose dogmas, but presents a path of intellectual and spiritual ascent. Careful reading will reveal that each concept presented here is not just a theoretical construct, but a key to perceiving an order that underlies everyday experience.

May this work serve the reader as an invitation to contemplation and questioning, as a philosophical and spiritual exercise. Because to know this invisible structure of reality is, ultimately, to begin the path back to the primordial source.

Luiz Santos, Editor

Chapter 1
The Philosophical Context of Neoplatonism

Neoplatonism emerges as a philosophical current in the 3rd century AD, a period of intense transformations in the Hellenistic and Roman world. To fully understand Neoplatonism, it is necessary to situate it within its specific historical context, exploring the social, political, and intellectual conditions that fostered its flourishing. This was not a spontaneous birth, but rather the result of a long process of confluence and development of diverse traditions of thought that intertwined over the centuries.

The world in which Neoplatonism manifests is the world of the late Roman Empire, a vast and cosmopolitan empire which, despite its apparent solidity, was already beginning to feel the internal and external pressures that would eventually lead to its transformation. The Pax Romana, a period of relative stability and prosperity that marked the first centuries of the empire, was beginning to give way to a more unstable scenario, marked by political, economic, and social crises. Civil wars, barbarian invasions, and the increasing complexity of imperial administration created a climate of uncertainty and questioning about traditional values and institutions.

Within this context of change, philosophical currents played a crucial role in the intellectual and spiritual life of the time. Philosophy was not seen merely as an academic discipline, but as a path to wisdom, virtue, and, in many cases, to personal salvation. Philosophical schools offered systems of thought that sought to give meaning to human existence, answer the great questions of metaphysics and ethics, and provide a guide to a full and meaningful life.

Neoplatonism largely emerges as an heir and continuator of the Greek philosophical tradition, particularly the thought of Plato. Plato's influence is absolutely central to Neoplatonism, and its main exponents considered themselves interpreters and continuators of the true Platonic doctrine. However, Neoplatonism is not limited to being a mere repetition of classical Platonism. It incorporates and transforms elements from other philosophical schools, such as Pythagoreanism and Aristotelianism, as well as influences from religious and mystical currents of the Hellenistic and Eastern world.

Pythagoreanism, with its emphasis on mathematics, cosmic harmony, and the immortality of the soul, left a profound mark on Neoplatonism. The idea that reality is structured according to mathematical principles and that the order of the cosmos reflects a fundamental harmony is a central idea of both Pythagoreanism and Neoplatonism. Similarly, the belief in the pre-existence and immortality of the soul, as well as the quest for purification and liberation from the cycle of reincarnations, are themes that Neoplatonism inherits and develops from the Pythagorean tradition.

Aristotelianism also exerted a significant, albeit more complex and nuanced influence. If, on the one hand, Neoplatonism distances itself from some of Aristotle's central theses, such as his conception of the soul as the form of the body and his emphasis on empirical observation as a method of knowledge, on the other hand, it incorporates elements of Aristotelian logic, metaphysics, and ethics. Aristotelian logic, in particular, was used by Neoplatonists to develop complex and rigorous arguments in defense of their doctrines. Aristotle's metaphysics, with its distinction between act and potency, form and matter, also provided a vocabulary and conceptual framework that were adapted and transformed by Neoplatonism. In ethics, the Aristotelian ideal of the virtuous life and the pursuit of happiness as the realization of human potential also resonates, albeit in a transfigured form, in Neoplatonic thought.

Beyond Greek philosophical influences, Neoplatonism also absorbed elements from religious and mystical currents that circulated in the Hellenistic world. Hermetism, Gnosticism, and Eastern mystery religions, such as the cult of Isis and Mithras, contributed themes and images that were integrated into the Neoplatonic system. The emphasis on divine transcendence, the importance of revelation and mystical experience, and the quest for union with the divine are aspects that reflect these influences. It is important to note, however, that Neoplatonism is not limited to being a religious syncretism. It seeks to integrate these influences within a coherent and rational philosophical system, maintaining its identity as a school of philosophical thought.

The main centers of development of Neoplatonism were Alexandria, Rome, and Athens. Alexandria, in Egypt, was an important cultural and intellectual center of the Hellenistic world, famous for its library and museum. It was in Alexandria that Plotinus, considered the founder of Neoplatonism, began his philosophical activity in the 3rd century AD. Rome also became an important center of Neoplatonism, attracting philosophers and intellectuals from various parts of the empire. In Athens, the ancient philosophical capital of Greece, Neoplatonism flourished in the 4th and 5th centuries AD, with the foundation of an important philosophical school that continued the Platonic tradition until the 6th century AD, when it was closed by Emperor Justinian.

Neoplatonism, therefore, cannot be understood as an isolated phenomenon, but as a sophisticated and deeply rooted response to the tensions of its time. While preserving the Greek philosophical heritage, it adapts to the new spiritual and intellectual anxieties of a society in transformation, which sought both rational explanations for the order of the cosmos and paths of personal salvation in the face of the fragility of earthly existence. This ability to reconcile tradition and innovation, reason and mysticism, contributed to Neoplatonism becoming a powerful and influential synthesis, capable of dialoguing with different currents of thought and religiosity.

This openness to dialogue, however, did not mean loss of philosophical identity. Neoplatonists maintained the conviction that philosophy, more than a speculative exercise, was a spiritual practice aimed at the transformation of the soul and ascension to the One, the supreme and ineffable principle of all reality. The search for contemplation of this ultimate principle unified their metaphysical, ethical, and epistemological reflections, giving Neoplatonism a rare internal coherence amidst the intellectual syncretism of the time. Each concept, each practice, and each textual interpretation was oriented by this greater horizon, in which knowing was, at the same time, becoming, and understanding meant participating in divine being itself.

In this way, Neoplatonism consolidated itself as a philosophical synthesis that not only preserved the Platonic tradition in times of uncertainty, but also offered an intellectual and spiritual itinerary for those seeking meaning and transcendence. Its influence far surpassed the borders of the ancient world, nourishing medieval philosophy, Renaissance thought, and various esoteric and mystical currents throughout the centuries. By integrating philosophical rationality and spiritual yearning, Neoplatonism built a lasting bridge between Greek thought and the great religious and philosophical traditions that shaped the West.

Chapter 2
Neoplatonic Thought

Neoplatonic thought rests on a set of metaphysical and cosmological principles that distinguish it from other philosophical currents of antiquity and that form the basis for its understanding of hypostases and the soul's journey towards the divine. These foundations, although complex and interconnected, can be understood through the analysis of key concepts that permeate the entire architecture of the Neoplatonic system. Reality as emanation from the One, divine transcendence and immanence, and the importance of contemplation and the ascetic journey constitute essential pillars for entering the intellectual universe of Neoplatonism.

Neoplatonic metaphysics postulates that reality, in all its vastness and complexity, derives from a primordial and transcendent source which is the One. The One, also called the Good or the First Principle, is not simply the highest entity within a hierarchy of beings, but rather the very condition of possibility of all existence. It is radically simple, indivisible, and perfect, transcending all categories of being and thought. The One cannot be defined or circumscribed by concepts, as any definition would imply a limitation and, therefore, an imperfection. It is beyond being and non-being, finite and infinite, time and eternity. Language, by its discursive and categorical nature, is intrinsically inadequate to express the nature of the One, which can only be apprehended through a direct and immediate intellectual intuition.

The relationship between the One and the rest of reality is understood through the concept of emanation. Emanation is not creation in the traditional sense, that is, an act of will by a creator that brings something into existence from nothing. Instead, emanation is conceived as a necessary and spontaneous process, similar to the overflowing of an inexhaustible spring. The One, in its fullness and perfection, radiates reality out of itself, not by diminishing or losing its own essence, but by pure superabundance. The emanations that proceed from the One are not separate or distinct from it, but rather gradual and differentiated manifestations of its primordial unity. Reality emanates from the One as light emanates from the sun, or as fragrance emanates from a flower.

The first emanation from the One is the Intellect (Nous), also known as the Logos or the Divine Mind. The Intellect is the domain of pure thought and Platonic Forms, the eternal and immutable archetypes of all things that exist in the sensible world. While the One is simple and undivided, the Intellect is characterized by duality and multiplicity. It contains within itself the thought of itself and the thought of the One, reflecting, in a way, the unity of the One, but already in the form of subject-object distinction. The Intellect is the place of perfect intelligibility, where all Forms are eternally present and knowable. It is the paradigm of knowledge and the source of reason and order in the universe.

From the Intellect, emanates the Soul (Psyché), which is the third primordial hypostasis. The Soul is the animating and organizing principle of the sensible world. It unfolds into the World Soul, which governs and animates the cosmos as a whole, and into individual souls, which inhabit the bodies of living beings. The Soul is characterized by its capacity for movement and change, and by its ambiguous relationship with the intelligible world and the sensible world. While the Intellect remains fixed in the contemplation of the Forms, the Soul turns to the material world, seeking to order and give form to formless matter. It is a mediator between the divine and the sensible world, and is responsible for the order, beauty, and harmony that manifest in the cosmos.

The doctrine of hypostases, which will be explored in detail in subsequent chapters, constitutes the backbone of Neoplatonic cosmology and metaphysics. The hypostases represent gradual levels of divine reality, each emanating from the previous one and, at the same time, aspiring to return to its primordial source. This dynamic of emanation and return, also known as procession (próodos) and conversion (epistrophé), is fundamental to understanding the journey of the soul and the search for union with the divine in Neoplatonism.

Divine transcendence is a central concept in Neoplatonic thought. The One, as the primordial source of all reality, absolutely transcends the sensible world and even the intelligible world. It is not a being among other beings, not even the supreme being, but rather the transcendental condition of all being. The transcendence of the One implies its ineffability and unknowability. We cannot apprehend the One through the senses or discursive reason, but only through an intellectual intuition that transcends conceptual thought. Language, by its finite and categorical nature, is always inadequate to express the infinity and simplicity of the One. Neoplatonic theology is, therefore, predominantly apophatic, that is, characterized by the negation of all positive attributes in relation to the divine. Saying what God is not becomes more meaningful than trying to say what He is.

Despite the emphasis on transcendence, Neoplatonism also recognizes divine immanence in the world. Although the One remains transcendent and ineffable, its presence manifests at all levels of reality through its emanations. The sensible world, although distant from the perfection of the One, is not deprived of its presence. The World Soul, as an emanation of the Intellect and the One, penetrates and animates the entire cosmos, conferring order, beauty, and intelligibility upon it. The divine presence in the world can be recognized through the contemplation of cosmic order and harmony, as well as through the beauty and perfection that manifest in natural forms. Divine immanence does not contradict transcendence, but rather complements it, revealing the mysterious and omnipresent presence of the divine in all things.

Contemplation and the ascetic journey play a fundamental role in Neoplatonic philosophy as paths to union with the divine. Contemplation, in the Neoplatonic sense, is not merely an act of discursive thought or conceptual analysis, but rather a direct and immediate intellectual intuition that transcends rational thought. Through contemplation, the soul elevates itself above the sensible world and discursive thought, and turns to the intelligible world, seeking to apprehend the Forms and, ultimately, the One itself. Contemplation is a spiritual exercise that requires discipline, purification, and concentration, and that aims to lead the soul to a state of ecstasy and mystical union with the divine.

The ascetic journey, in turn, is the practical path of purification and preparation of the soul for contemplation and union. It involves renunciation of sensible pleasures and material attachments, the cultivation of moral and intellectual virtues, and the practice of spiritual exercises such as meditation and prayer. The ascetic journey is not seen as an end in itself, but rather as a means to liberate the soul from its passions and illusions, and to make it fit to receive divine illumination. The purification of the soul is essential for its return to its divine origin, and ascetic practice is the path that leads to this purification.

In this intricate metaphysical edifice, Neoplatonic thought reveals its profound conviction that reality is, ultimately, an incessant movement of return to primordial unity. Each level of existence, from the Intellect to incarnated souls, participates in this longing for reintegration, as if the entire structure of the cosmos were moved by an original longing, an ancestral memory of lost fullness. Thus, the spiritual journey of the individual is not an isolated adventure, but a microcosmic expression of a universal dynamism that permeates all things—the innate search for reunion with the Source, whose subtle, yet insistent presence, echoes in every fragment of the sensible world.

This conception of reality, at once hierarchical and dynamic, imprints Neoplatonic thought with a mark of rigor and hope. Rigor, because it demands of the soul discipline, detachment, and an incessant polishing of itself so that it can ascend the steps of being to the contemplative vision of the divine. Hope, because the very fact of existing implies a common origin and, therefore, the promise of a possible return. The soul's itinerary, with its falls and ascensions, is not an arbitrary condemnation, but an opportunity to recover its true nature, rediscover its place in the fabric of the intelligible, and participate in the beatitude that emanates from the One.

In this way, Neoplatonic thought is not limited to an abstract speculation about first principles or the structure of the cosmos, but offers a worldview where philosophy merges with practical spirituality. By reconciling ontology and mysticism, reason and ecstasy, it transforms the philosophical exercise into a path of salvation, where knowing and being become faces of the same act. This fusion between intellectual contemplation and moral asceticism forges an integrated vision of existence, where the ultimate destiny of the soul is not only to understand the divine, but to become one with it, dissolving, finally, into the luminous silence of the Origin.

Chapter 3
The Concept of Hypostases

In the philosophical edifice of Neoplatonism, the concept of hypostasis occupies a central position, configuring itself as the keystone that sustains its cosmology, metaphysics, and soteriology. To delve into the complexity of Neoplatonic thought, it becomes essential to understand the nature and significance of hypostases, the levels of divine reality that emanate from the One and that constitute the fundamental structure of being. The word "hypostasis," with its rich and multifaceted semantic load, refers to the very essence of divine reality as conceived by the Neoplatonists, revealing the hierarchy, procession, and interconnection of the various levels of existence.

The etymology of the word "hypostasis" sheds light on its philosophical meaning. Derived from the Greek ὑπόστασις (hypóstasis), the word is composed of ὑπό (hypó), which means "under," "beneath," "foundation," and στάσις (stásis), which refers to "to stand," "to remain," "to subsist." Literally, hypostasis can be translated as "that which stands under," "what underlies," "the foundation," "the underlying substance." In the philosophical context, hypostasis acquires the sense of "substantial reality," "real entity," "mode of being," "level of existence." Employed within the scope of Neoplatonism, the word hypostasis designates the various levels of divine reality that emanate from the One, each with its own substance, mode of being, and function within the economy of reality.

In the Neoplatonic system, hypostases are understood as distinct levels of divine reality, each deriving from the previous one in a descending progression that starts from the One, the primordial and transcendent source of all being. This hierarchy of hypostases should not be understood as a mere scale of values or an arbitrary organization, but rather as an expression of the very ontological structure of reality, which unfolds and manifests itself in different degrees of perfection and complexity. Hypostases are not separate and independent entities, but rather differentiated moments or aspects of a single and same divine reality, united by a bond of emanation and participation.

The hierarchy of hypostases is typically presented in a fundamental triad, composed of the One, the Intellect (Nous), and the Soul (Psyché). These three primary hypostases represent the highest and most fundamental levels of divine reality, constituting the basis for the emanation of all other levels of existence. The One, as already explored in the previous chapter, is the supreme hypostasis, the ineffable and unknowable source of all reality. From it emanates the Intellect, the second hypostasis, which is the domain of pure thought, of Platonic Forms, and of divine intelligence. From the Intellect, in turn, emanates the Soul, the third hypostasis, which is the animating and organizing principle of the sensible world, mediating between the intelligible world and the material world.

Beyond the primordial triad, late Neoplatonism, particularly in the works of Proclus and Iamblichus, developed and expanded the hierarchy of hypostases, introducing an even greater number of levels of divine reality, including the Aeons, Archangels, Demons, and other intermediary entities. This complexification of the hierarchy of hypostases reflects an attempt to account for the richness and diversity of manifest reality, as well as to explain the various degrees of mediation between the transcendent One and the sensible world. The Aeons, in particular, acquire a prominent role in late Neoplatonism, configuring themselves as intermediary levels of divine reality that play a crucial role in Neoplatonic cosmology and soteriology.

The order of hypostases is not only hierarchical, but also processional. This means that hypostases emanate from each other in a continuous stream of reality, starting from the One and descending towards multiplicity and materiality. This procession is not a spatial or temporal movement, but rather an ontological emanation, a derivation of being from being, of perfection from perfection, of unity from unity. Each hypostasis, upon emanating from the previous one, preserves in itself the essence of its source, but at the same time manifests a certain differentiation and complexification, resulting in a progressive decrease in perfection and unity as it distances itself from the One.

Despite their hierarchical and processional order, hypostases are not separate or isolated from each other, but rather interconnected and interdependent. Each hypostasis participates in the reality of those that precede it and, at the same time, serves as a foundation for those that succeed it. There is a continuity and constant communication between hypostases, such that divine reality manifests itself at all levels of existence, albeit in diverse and gradual ways. This interconnection of hypostases reflects the fundamental unity of divine reality, which, despite its multiplicity and differentiation, remains one and indivisible in its essence.

The understanding of the concept of hypostasis is fundamental to interpreting Neoplatonic cosmology. Hypostases provide the structural framework of the cosmos, defining the different levels of reality that compose it and their mutual relations. The Neoplatonic cosmos is not a homogeneous and undifferentiated universe, but rather a hierarchical and organic system, ordered according to the emanation of hypostases. Each level of the cosmos, from the intelligible world to the sensible world, corresponds to one or more hypostases, reflecting their nature and characteristics. The cosmic order, therefore, is a manifestation of the divine order, and the understanding of the structure of hypostases is essential to understanding the order of the cosmos.

Beyond cosmology, the concept of hypostasis also plays a crucial role in Neoplatonic soteriology, that is, in the doctrine of salvation or liberation of the soul. The soul's journey towards the One is understood as a process of ascension through the hypostases, a gradual return to the primordial source of all reality. The human soul, in its essence, is akin to the higher hypostases, particularly to the World Soul and the Intellect, and its ultimate goal is to transcend its material condition and unite with the One, realizing its full spiritual potential. This ascension of the soul through the hypostases is achieved through the practice of philosophy, contemplation, purification, and virtue, in a gradual and laborious process that requires effort, discipline, and divine illumination.

Hypostases, therefore, do not only constitute a theoretical description of the structure of being, but delineate the very spiritual itinerary of the soul in its yearning to return to the primordial source. Each level of reality is, at the same time, a degree of remoteness and a possibility of ascension, a pale reflection of the original perfection and a path of reintegration into the whole. It is in this constant dialogue between emanation and return, between dispersion and unity, that the Neoplatonic spiritual experience is configured — a journey in which the knowledge of oneself and of the cosmos reveals itself inseparable from the reunion with the One.

This movement of return, far from being a simple passive contemplation, demands from the soul an active and transformative involvement. Ascending through the hypostases is not only intellectually understanding their nature, but submitting oneself to a slow purification, in which every tie with matter and with the illusions of multiplicity needs to be undone. The soul, reflecting in the imperfect mirror of the sensible world the traces of its origin, learns to read in the order of the cosmos the signs of the divine presence, until, finally, already stripped of the layers of otherness, it recognizes in its innermost center the same light that shines at the summit of the hierarchy of hypostases.

Thus, the concept of hypostases transcends the role of a simple metaphysical scheme and becomes an interpretative key to the very human condition. By describing the unfolding of being from the absolute simplicity of the One to the fragmented multiplicity of the material world, Neoplatonism offers the soul not only a map of reality, but a roadmap of return. In this double movement — of fall and of return, of separation and of reintegration — the soul rediscovers its divine vocation, understanding that its ultimate destiny is not to remain dispersed among the shadows of matter, but to reintegrate itself into the serene and silent light of primal unity.

Chapter 4
Divine Reality

The expression "divine reality," in the context of Neoplatonism, transcends common and sometimes limited notions of divinity present in other philosophical and religious traditions. For Neoplatonists, the divine is not restricted to a supreme being, a personal creator, or an anthropomorphic entity, but encompasses the totality of being, understood in its various levels and manifestations. Understanding the meaning of "divine reality" in Neoplatonism implies delving into a deep and complex metaphysical conception, which seeks to elucidate the nature of the divine beyond the categories of discursive thought and conceptual language. The Neoplatonic divine reveals itself as something simultaneously transcendent and immanent, ineffable and present, one and multiple, constituting the ultimate horizon of philosophical and spiritual seeking.

The nature of the divine in Neoplatonism is primarily characterized by its transcendence. The One, the supreme hypostasis and the source of all reality, radically transcends the sensible world and even the intelligible world. This transcendence does not refer merely to a hierarchical superiority or a spatial distance, but to a fundamental ontological difference. The One is beyond being and existence as we understand them, transcending all categories of thought and language. It is not an object of knowledge, but the condition of possibility of all knowledge; it is not a being among other beings, but the source of all being. The transcendence of the One implies its ineffability and incognoscibility. Any attempt to define the One, to attribute qualities or attributes to it, implies a limitation and, therefore, a misunderstanding of its true nature. Language, by its own finite and categorical structure, is inherently inadequate to express the infinity and simplicity of the One. Neoplatonic theology, consequently, adopts an apophatic path, a negative theology that seeks to approach the divine through the negation of all positive attributes, recognizing that the true divine is always beyond everything we can say or think about it.

This emphasis on transcendence does not imply, however, an absolute detachment of the divine from the world. If the One transcends all categories of being, it is also immanent in all reality, present at all levels of existence through its emanations. Divine immanence manifests itself in the order, beauty, and intelligibility of the cosmos, in the harmony and cohesion of the natural world, and in the mysterious and ineffable presence that permeates all things. The World Soul, in particular, as an emanation of the Intellect and the One, penetrates and animates the entire cosmos, endowing it with life, movement, and organization. The divine presence in the world is not a manifest and evident presence, but rather a veiled and mysterious presence, which reveals itself to those who are capable of contemplating the order and beauty of the cosmos with an attentive and perceptive gaze. Divine immanence, therefore, complements transcendence, revealing that the divine is not only beyond the world, but also present in it, as its source and foundation.

Within this perspective, Neoplatonism distinguishes between the transcendent divine and the manifest divine. The transcendent divine refers to the One in its absolute simplicity and ineffability, beyond all manifestation and differentiation. It is the divine in itself, in its ultimate and unfathomable nature. The manifest divine, in turn, refers to the emanations of the One, to the hypostases of the Intellect and the Soul, and to all levels of reality that proceed from the primordial source. The manifest divine is the divine that is revealed in the cosmos, that becomes present and knowable through its works and manifestations. The distinction between the transcendent divine and the manifest divine does not imply a duality or a separation, but rather a differentiation within the divine unity. The manifest divine is not something distinct or separate from the transcendent divine, but rather its expression and manifestation in the world. Just as light manifests the presence of the sun, the emanations of the One manifest the presence of the transcendent divine in the cosmos.

The objective of Neoplatonic philosophy, ultimately, is union with the divine. This union is not conceived as a fusion or annihilation of individuality, but as a realization of the full spiritual potential of the human soul, a return to its divine origin and a participation in the life and beatitude of the One. The soul's journey toward the divine is an ascetic and contemplative process, which involves the purification of passions and material attachments, the cultivation of moral and intellectual virtues, and the practice of meditation and intellectual contemplation. Through contemplation, the soul rises above the sensible world and discursive thought, and turns towards the intelligible world, seeking to apprehend the Forms and, ultimately, the One itself. Union with the divine is the supreme state of spiritual realization, the culminating point of the soul's journey, where it finds the peace, happiness, and fullness it seeks.

This union with the divine, in Neoplatonism, is not understood as a unique and definitive event, but as a continuous and dynamic process, an incessant search for perfection and transcendence. The human soul, even when it achieves mystical union, does not cease to be a soul, nor does it completely merge with the One. Union with the divine is more properly described as a participation in divine life, a communion with the One, a contemplation of its beauty and perfection. This participation, communion, and contemplation are not passive or static states, but rather dynamic and continuous activities, which nourish and transform the soul, bringing it ever closer to its divine source.

In this horizon, Neoplatonic divine reality reveals itself as a living fabric of relationships, in which each level of being, each hypostasis, and each individual soul participates, albeit in a veiled and fragmentary way, in the silent presence of the One. The divine is not found only at the inaccessible apex of transcendence, but permeates and sustains every instant, every form, and every gesture of cosmic reality. To contemplate this hidden presence is, for the Neoplatonic philosopher, to learn to read in the very being of the world the echo of its origin—an origin that does not impose itself, but invites, does not explain itself, but whispers through the order and beauty that pervade the cosmos.

This participation in the divine, however, does not occur automatically or spontaneously. The veil of multiplicity and matter obscures the primordial light, making the spiritual journey a path of effort and purification. For the human being, this search is not only intellectual, but existential: to know the divine implies transforming oneself, freeing oneself from the layers of forgetfulness and dispersion that imprison the soul in the shadows of the sensible. Philosophy, in this sense, is not just theoretical speculation, but a spiritual practice, a method of leading the soul back to its original clarity, where it can recognize itself as a reflection of the divine and a participant in eternity.

Thus, Neoplatonic divine reality is, at the same time, an unattainable mystery and an intimate presence, an inaccessible abyss and the very substance of the soul. This tension between the transcendent divine and the immanent divine is not a paradox to be resolved, but the very dynamic of existence, in which each being, in its degree of perfection or imperfection, is called to reflect the light of the One. Between dispersion and return, between the world and the divine, the soul walks—and it is in this walking that Neoplatonism finds its true heart: a philosophy that is, first and foremost, a way of returning to the primordial home.

Chapter 5
Absolute Transcendence

The One rises as the first hypostasis, the pinnacle of the hierarchy of being in the Neoplatonic system, representing the primordial source of all reality and the maximum expression of absolute transcendence. Beyond any category or concept that the human mind can conceive, the One remains ineffable and unknowable, constituting the ultimate mystery that permeates existence and reveals itself as the condition of possibility of all that is. Exploring the nature of the One implies entering a domain that defies language and discursive thought, requiring an approach that opens itself to intellectual intuition and silent contemplation. The understanding of the One is not achieved through definition or description, but through a progressive approximation, a recognition of its radical otherness and its unconditional transcendence.

The ineffable and unknowable nature of the One lies at the heart of Neoplatonic metaphysics. The One transcends all categories of being and non-being, of the finite and the infinite, of time and eternity. It cannot be adequately described as a "thing" or as a "being," as these categories imply limitations and determinations that are incompatible with its absolute simplicity and perfection. Any attribute that one might try to ascribe to the One, such as "good," "one," "perfect," is always inadequate and, ultimately, limiting. These attributes, when applied to the One, must be understood analogically and transcendently, not in the sense of qualities that define it, but as indications of its perfection and its preeminence in relation to all that we know. The ineffability of the One is not a deficiency or a limitation, but an expression of its transcendence and its superiority in relation to all language and all human thought. To try to describe the One with words would be like trying to imprison the ocean in a glass of water.

The unknowability of the One is a direct consequence of its ineffability. If language is inadequate to describe the One, discursive thought also proves powerless to apprehend it. Knowledge, as we understand it, implies a subject-object distinction, a relationship between the knower and the knowable. In the case of the One, this distinction dissolves, for the One is so radically simple and one that it cannot be an object of knowledge in the traditional sense. There is no "other" in relation to the One that can be known, and thought itself, in its dual and discursive nature, is incapable of reaching its simplicity and unity. Knowledge of the One is therefore not conceptual or discursive knowledge, but direct and immediate intellectual intuition, a mystical experience that transcends rational thought. This intuition, however, is not a complete or exhaustive apprehension of the One, but a fleeting and momentary glimpse of its transcendent reality, an intimate contact that leaves the soul ecstatic and transformed.

Despite its ineffability and unknowability, the One is the source of all reality, the primordial principle from which everything emanates and to which everything tends to return. The One is primordial unity, the root of all multiplicity, the origin of all differentiation. It is the foundation of being, the condition of possibility of all existence. Without the One, nothing could be, nothing could exist. Reality emanates from the One as light emanates from the sun, or as water springs from a source. This emanation is not an act of creation in the traditional sense, but a necessary and spontaneous process, a consequence of the superabundance and perfection of the One. The One, in its fullness, overflows reality out of itself, not through diminution or loss of its own essence, but through pure generosity and fecundity. The reality that emanates from the One is not separate or distinct from it, but a gradual and differentiated manifestation of its primordial unity, an expression of its richness and its fullness.

The concept of "procession" or emanation from the One is fundamental to understanding Neoplatonic cosmology. Procession describes the movement of reality from the One, its gradual descent through the different levels of existence, from the intelligible world to the sensible world. This process should not be understood as a fall or a degeneration, but as an unfolding or a manifestation of divine reality in different degrees of complexity and differentiation. Procession starts from the One, absolute and undivided unity, and moves towards multiplicity and differentiation, culminating in the sensible world, the level of reality furthest from the One. Each level of reality that emanates from the One preserves within itself the mark of its origin, but at the same time manifests a certain diminution of perfection and unity, resulting in a progressive complexification and materialization of reality.

Procession is not only a descending movement, but also an ascending movement, a return to the primordial source. The human soul, in its essence, participates in divine nature and aspires to return to the One, to union with its primordial origin. This return is achieved through the ascetic and contemplative journey, a process of purification and spiritual elevation that aims to free the soul from its passions and illusions, and make it fit to receive divine illumination and unite with the One. The journey of the soul is, therefore, a circular movement, starting from the One, descending through procession, and returning to the One through conversion. This cycle of procession and conversion is the fundamental dynamic of reality in the Neoplatonic system, revealing unity and multiplicity, transcendence and immanence, distance and return to the divine source.

In this cosmic cycle of emanation and return, the One remains as the unmoved mystery that, without losing its simplicity, allows the unfolding of all the complexity of being. It is not only the first term in a causal chain, but the very silent foundation that makes existence possible in its totality. Each soul that walks the path of spiritual ascent, each intellect that seeks to understand the order of the cosmos, participates, albeit imperfectly, in this primordial impulse of return to the One. The One is, at the same time, that which can never be fully achieved and that which secretly inhabits each being, like a distant memory that draws all things back to their origin.

This double movement—procession that multiplies and conversion that reunites—is the secret rhythm of reality in Neoplatonic thought. Even in moments of greatest dispersion, in the fragmented world of matter and the sensible, pulsates the nostalgia for that lost unity, the silent memory of the One that sustains the innate desire for reunion. This desire, far from being just an individual aspiration, is the very dynamic of the cosmos, for everything that exists, however distant it may be, carries within it a spark of that primordial unity, a faint reflection of the light that never ceases to illuminate being.

The absolute transcendence of the One, therefore, does not mean absence or indifference in relation to what emanates from it. On the contrary, it is this transcendence that allows the One to be present without dissolving, to be the origin without being captured, to remain untouched even while it generates and sustains all things. The One is that which invites, but never forces; that calls from within and from without, and that can only be rediscovered when the soul, emptied of all inferior desire, recognizes that its true nature is only a shadow projected by the light of the ineffable.

Chapter 6
The Emanation of Divine Thought

Emerging directly from the transcendental unity of the One, the Intellect, or Nous, manifests itself as the first and most sublime emanation, the perfect mirror that reflects the ineffable perfection of its source. In the Neoplatonic system, the Intellect occupies a position of eminence, configuring itself as the domain of divine thought, the realm of Platonic Forms, and the seat of cosmic intelligence. To understand the Intellect, it is essential to delve into the universe of pure thought, unveiling its nature, its characteristics, and its fundamental role in the architecture of divine reality. The Intellect is not only an emanation of the One, but also an essential mediator between absolute transcendence and the multiplicity of manifest reality, constituting a vital link in the chain of being.

The Intellect emerges as the first emanation of the One, the first unfolding of primordial unity. While the One remains in its absolute and undivided simplicity, the Intellect represents the beginning of differentiation, the awakening of divine consciousness. This emanation should not be understood as a separation or division from the One, but rather as a manifestation of its inner richness, an expansion of its perfection towards multiplicity. The Intellect remains intrinsically linked to its source, preserving within itself the mark of primordial unity, but at the same time manifesting a new dimension of divine reality, the dimension of thought and intelligence. The relationship between the One and the Intellect is often compared to the relationship between the sun and light: light emanates from the sun, manifesting its luminous nature, but remains inseparable from its source, participating in its essence.

The Intellect is understood as the domain of divine thought, the cosmic mind that contains within itself the totality of knowledge and intelligence. This thought is not discursive or sequential, like human thought, but rather a pure and immediate thought, an intellectual intuition that simultaneously encompasses the totality of intelligible reality. The Intellect thinks itself and thinks the One, constituting an act of divine self-consciousness and contemplation of its primordial source. This thought is eternal and immutable, always present and always perfect, reflecting the eternal and immutable nature of the One itself. The Intellect is the place of absolute truth, where all things are known perfectly and immediately, without a shadow of error or illusion. It is the paradigm of knowledge and the source of all intelligence and rationality that manifest in the universe.

Within the Intellect resides the realm of Platonic Forms, the eternal and immutable archetypes of all things that exist in the sensible world. Forms are the perfect and universal essences of particular entities, the ideal models according to which the material world is configured. Beauty itself, Justice itself, Goodness itself, Man itself, Horse itself, and so on, are Forms that exist in the Intellect, eternal and immutable, perfect and universal. Sensible things, in turn, participate in the Forms, imperfectly and transiently imitating them. Sensible beauty participates in the Form of Beauty, human justice participates in the Form of Justice, and so on. Forms are, therefore, the foundation of intelligible reality and the model for sensible reality. They are the object of true knowledge and the source of order and intelligibility in the universe.

The relationship of the Intellect with truth, beauty, and goodness is intrinsic and essential. The Intellect is the domain of truth, for it contains within itself the perfect knowledge of all things, the Platonic Forms, which are the true and immutable essences of reality. Truth, for the Neoplatonists, is not merely a correspondence between thought and sensible reality, but rather an intellectual apprehension of the Forms, an intuition of the order and intelligibility that permeate the universe. The Intellect is also the domain of beauty, for the Platonic Forms are not only true, but also beautiful, manifesting the perfection and harmony of intelligible reality. Beauty, in this sense, is not merely an aesthetic or sensory quality, but rather an expression of order, proportion, and harmony that reflect divine perfection. The Intellect, finally, is intimately linked to goodness, for the One, source of the Intellect, is frequently identified with the supreme Good, the ultimate principle of all perfection and all goodness. Forms, as emanations of the One, participate in this primordial goodness, manifesting it in different degrees and modalities. Truth, beauty, and goodness are, therefore, interconnected and inseparable dimensions of the Intellect, expressions of its divine nature and its intrinsic perfection.

The Intellect, as the second hypostasis, occupies a mediating position between the transcendent One and the Soul, the third hypostasis, which turns towards the sensible world. The Intellect receives the light of the One and transmits it to the Soul, illuminating and guiding it in its task of ordering and animating the cosmos. The Soul, in turn, turns to the Intellect in search of knowledge and inspiration, contemplating the Forms and aspiring to union with the divine. This relationship between the Intellect and the Soul reflects the fundamental dynamic of Neoplatonic reality, the movement of procession and conversion, the descent of reality from the One and the return of the soul to its primordial source. The Intellect serves as a beacon for the soul, guiding it on its ascetic and contemplative journey, and offering it a glimpse of the beauty and perfection of the intelligible world.

In the foundations of the Intellect rests not only the architecture of divine thought, but also the pulsation of a cosmic order that permeates all levels of existence. Each Form contained therein is not an abstract concept or a distant mold of sensible reality, but a living presence, an expression of divine intelligence that echoes in the contours of the material world. In contemplating the Intellect, the soul not only knows, but recognizes itself—it intuits in the reflection of these Forms the memory of its origin and the promise of its return. Thus, the Intellect is not only a source of knowledge; it is a mirror and a call, a silent voice that invites the soul to reconstitute in itself primordial harmony.

This contemplative movement, however, does not occur as a simple act of passive observation. It requires of the soul an inner conversion, an awakening that is only possible by detaching itself from the shadows and illusions of the sensible world. In the Intellect, knowledge and existence coincide, and to know is to become that which is contemplated. In seeking the Forms, the soul rediscovers its own essence, for the same light that illuminates the eternal archetypes pulses silently in its innermost center. The journey towards the Intellect is, therefore, a journey of return: each glimpse of eternal truth awakens forgotten echoes of the divine memory that the soul carries from its first breath.

The Intellect, thus, is not merely a metaphysical instance, but the luminous horizon of all spiritual seeking. It is the abode of truth, but also the path and the criterion of ascension. Between the unattainable One and the incessant flow of multiplicity, it remains as a pillar of stability, sustaining cosmic order and offering the soul dispersed in time the promise of reunion with its source. Each return to the Intellect is, therefore, an act of reconciliation between what we are and what we are truly called to be—a crossing from the sensible to the intelligible, from fragmentation to unity, from opacity to the primal clarity of divine thought.

Chapter 7
The Connection with the Sensible World

Emerging from the Intellect, the Soul, or Psyché, manifests itself as the third primary hypostasis in the Neoplatonic system, occupying a crucial place in cosmology and philosophical anthropology. The Soul is configured as the bridge between the intelligible world and the sensible world, the animating and organizing principle that permeates the cosmos and connects divine reality with the materiality of existence. To understand the Soul, it is essential to explore its mediating nature, its role in animating the world, and its complex relationship with individual souls and the human body. The Soul is not merely a vital principle, but a complex cosmic entity, endowed with intelligence, will, and desire, which plays a fundamental role in the order of the universe and in the journey of the human soul towards its divine origin.

The Soul arises as an emanation of the Intellect, deriving its existence and its characteristics from the second primary hypostasis. Just as the Intellect emanates from the One, the Soul emanates from the Intellect, in a continuous process of unfolding and manifestation of divine reality. While the Intellect remains fixed in the contemplation of the Forms and in the unity of divine thought, the Soul turns to the external world, to the multiplicity and diversity of sensible reality. This emanation does not imply a separation or a fall of the Soul in relation to the Intellect, but rather an expansion of its activity and its influence, a manifestation of its capacity to give form and order to formless matter. The Soul retains within itself the mark of its intellectual origin, participating in the intelligence and rationality of the Intellect, but at the same time manifesting new qualities and capacities, such as motility, sensibility, and imagination.

The Soul plays the role of essential mediator between the intelligible world and the sensible world, between divine reality and material reality. It is situated at an intermediate point in the hierarchy of being, connecting the upper and lower levels of existence. On the one hand, the Soul turns to the Intellect, contemplating the Forms and receiving divine illumination. On the other hand, it turns to the sensible world, giving it form, order, and life. This mediating function of the Soul is crucial to Neoplatonic cosmology, as it ensures communication and interaction between the different levels of reality, preventing the intelligible world and the sensible world from becoming completely separate and isolated. The Soul is like a mirror that reflects the light of the Intellect to the material world, making it intelligible and ordered, and at the same time, it elevates the sensible world towards the intelligible, awakening in sensible creatures the desire for knowledge and union with the divine.

In the Neoplatonic system, a distinction is made between the World Soul (Anima Mundi) and individual souls. The World Soul is the cosmic soul, the animating and organizing principle of the universe as a whole. It penetrates and animates the entire cosmos, from celestial bodies to terrestrial living beings, conferring upon it movement, life, and order. The World Soul is responsible for the harmony and beauty of the cosmos, for the regularity of celestial movements, for the succession of seasons, for the diversity of living species, and for the interconnection of all parts of the universe. It is the source of life and intelligence in the cosmos, the unifying principle that keeps the universe cohesive and ordered. The World Soul is not an entity separate from the cosmos, but rather its own soul, its intrinsic vital force, the principle that animates and governs it from within.

Individual souls, in turn, are emanations or parts of the World Soul, which individualize and incarnate in the bodies of living beings, particularly in human beings. Each individual soul retains within itself the nature of the World Soul, participating in its intelligence, its will, and its capacity to love. However, individual souls are also limited and obscured by their union with the material body, which distances them from their divine origin and plunges them into the world of passions and sensible illusions. Despite this limited condition, individual souls retain the capacity to turn to their divine origin, to recall their spiritual nature, and to seek union with the Intellect and the One. The journey of the human soul, in Neoplatonism, is understood as a process of liberation from the shackles of the body and the material world, a gradual return to its divine origin, and a realization of its full spiritual potentiality.

The role of the Soul in the animation and order of the cosmos is multifaceted and comprehensive. It is responsible for conferring life and movement to all living beings, from the simplest to the most complex. It is also responsible for the order and harmony of the cosmos, for the regularity of natural phenomena, and for the intelligent organization of the universe. The Soul acts as a modeling and organizing force, giving form to formless matter and transforming chaos into cosmos. It imprints on the material world the intelligible Forms that it contemplated in the Intellect, manifesting the beauty, order, and intelligibility of divine reality in the sensible world. The Soul is, therefore, the active principle that makes the universe alive, ordered, and knowable, revealing the presence and action of divine intelligence in all parts of the cosmos.

The Soul, in its mediating and animating function, is intrinsically linked to the sensible world, but also maintains an essential relationship with the intelligible world. It is simultaneously turned downwards, towards the material world that it animates and orders, and turned upwards, towards the Intellect and the One, which are its origin and ultimate goal. This dual orientation of the Soul reflects its ambiguous nature and its intermediate position in the hierarchy of being. It is the frontier between the divine and the material, the meeting point between the intelligible and the sensible, the link that unites the different levels of reality. The

Soul is, therefore, a dynamic and complex principle, which plays a fundamental role in Neoplatonic cosmology, anthropology, and soteriology.

It is in the constant tension between these two faces—the contemplative and the creative—that the Soul fulfills its true cosmic function. By contemplating the eternal Forms in the Intellect, it absorbs the immutable models of order and beauty; by turning to matter, it imprints on these invisible forms the vital breath that animates and structures the sensible world. This incessant dance between contemplation and creation, between the intelligible heaven and the sensible earth, makes the Soul not only a mediator, but the silent artificer of a cosmos where each being carries in its constitution the echo of a superior harmony. Even in the densest material body, the Soul whispers the memory of its celestial origin.

However, upon descending to the sensible plane, the Soul does not escape the limitations and challenges imposed by matter. Each form that it animates is also a partial prison, a layer of opacity that veiledly obscures the pure light of the Intellect. Individual souls, in particular, live this contradiction more acutely: they inhabit bodies that restrict them, desires that disperse them, memories that confuse them. But it is precisely in this intermediate condition, between the fleeting brightness of matter and the fullness of the intelligible, that their greatest potency resides. At every instant, even immersed in shadows, they retain the capacity to remember and return, to convert dispersion into recollection and fragmentation into unity.

The Soul, therefore, not only animates and orders the cosmos, but imprints upon it the very possibility of redemption. Through its presence in bodies and in the cycles of nature, it draws invisible paths that point towards ascension and towards reunion with the divine. Even while modeling and governing the multiplicity of the sensible world, the Soul preserves in its movement an ultimate direction: not mere permanence in the flow of time and matter, but final reintegration into the luminous bosom of the Intellect and, through it, into the silent simplicity of the One. Each being that it animates is, in essence, a spark of this promise, a small flame destined to rediscover the primordial light that made it burn.

Chapter 8
One, Intellect, and Soul

Delving deeply into the architecture of the Neoplatonic being, it becomes essential to discern the characteristics and attributes that define and distinguish the three primary hypostases: the One, the Intellect, and the Soul. Although united by a bond of emanation and participation, each hypostasis manifests its own nature and function within the system of divine reality. The comparative analysis of the attributes of the One, the Intellect, and the Soul reveals the progressive differentiation and complexification of reality as it emanates from its primordial source, as well as the underlying unity that permeates the entire hierarchy of being. Understanding the specific characteristics of each hypostasis is fundamental to grasping the dynamics of emanation and return, and to tracing the soul's path towards union with the divine.

The One, as the first hypostasis, primarily manifests through its simplicity. This simplicity does not merely refer to the absence of complexity, but to its radical indivisibility, to its absolute unity that precedes all differentiation. The One is one not only in number but in essence, transcending all multiplicity and composition. Flowing from its simplicity emerges its transcendence. The One transcends all categories of being and thought, situated beyond any definition or concept that the human mind can conceive. This transcendence does not imply detachment, but rather a supereminence, a perfection that infinitely surpasses finite comprehension. The unity of the One, already mentioned, is another fundamental attribute. It is the source of the unity of all things, the unifying principle that underlies the diversity of the universe. Everything that exists participates in the unity of the One, albeit in gradual and differentiated ways. Ineffability also characterizes the One. Its ultimate nature escapes language and discursive thought, capable of being apprehended only through an intellectual intuition that transcends reason. Words, by their finite and categorical nature, are always inadequate to express the infinity and simplicity of the One. Finally, the One is the source. It is the origin of all reality, the primordial principle from which everything emanates and to which everything tends to return. Without the One, nothing could exist; it is the condition of possibility of all existence.

The Intellect, as the second hypostasis, manifests attributes that, although derived from the One, already express a certain differentiation and complexification. The primary attribute of the Intellect is thought. It is the domain of divine thought, of pure intelligence and cosmic consciousness. This thought is not discursive or sequential, but rather immediate and comprehensive, simultaneously intuiting the totality of intelligible reality. The Intellect thinks itself and thinks the One, constituting an act of divine self-consciousness and of contemplation of its primordial source. The Forms, already mentioned, constitute the content of the Intellect's thought. They are the eternal and immutable archetypes of all things, the perfect and universal essences that serve as models for sensible reality. The Intellect is the place of perfect intelligibility, where the Forms are eternally present and knowable. Duality or multiplicity in unity characterizes the Intellect in contrast to the absolute simplicity of the One. While the One is undivided, the Intellect manifests a fundamental duality, the thought of itself and the thought of the One, and contains within itself the multiplicity of the Forms. This multiplicity, however, remains unified by the divine intelligence of the Intellect. Intelligibility is another essential attribute of the Intellect. It is the domain of reason and order, the place where reality becomes knowable and comprehensible. The Intellect radiates intelligibility to the lower levels of reality, making the cosmos ordered and capable of being known by the human mind. Finally, the Intellect is intrinsically linked to the transcendental values of truth, beauty, and goodness. It is the place of absolute truth, where the Forms manifest their perfection and their intelligibility. It is also the domain of intelligible beauty, of harmony and proportion that reflect the divine order. And finally, it participates in the primordial goodness of the One, manifesting it through the perfection of the Forms and the order of the cosmos.

The Soul, as the third hypostasis, manifests attributes that distinguish it from the One and the Intellect, revealing its mediating function and its connection to the sensible world. The fundamental attribute of the Soul is movement. While the One remains unmoved in its transcendence and the Intellect rests in the eternal contemplation of the Forms, the Soul is characterized by its capacity for movement and change. This movement manifests in the animation of the cosmos, in the movement of celestial bodies, in the growth of living beings, and in the actions of individual souls. Animation is another essential attribute of the Soul. It is the animating principle that confers life and vitality to the cosmos and to living beings. The World Soul animates the universe as a whole, while individual souls animate the bodies of living beings. Mediation, already mentioned, defines the Soul's function in the hierarchy of being. It is the link between the intelligible world and the sensible world, the mediator between the divine and the material. The Soul transmits the light of the Intellect to the sensible world, making it ordered and intelligible, and elevates the sensible world towards the intelligible, awakening the desire for knowledge and for union with the divine. The connection with the sensible world is a distinctive characteristic of the Soul. While the One and the Intellect are situated in the purely intelligible domain, the Soul turns towards the sensible world, taking interest in its order, its beauty, and its life. This connection with the sensible world does not imply a fall or a degeneration of the Soul, but rather an expansion of its activity and its influence beyond the intelligible domain. Finally, the Soul manifests a lower level of intelligibility in comparison with the Intellect. Although it participates in divine intelligence, the Soul turns towards the sensible world, dealing with multiplicity and change, which implies a certain diminution of the purity and perfection of intellectual intelligence. The intelligence of the Soul is more discursive and practical, aimed at the organization and government of the sensible world, while the intelligence of the Intellect is purely contemplative and theoretical, aimed at the apprehension of the Forms and the One.

One, Intellect, and Soul thus form a continuous current where primordial unity unfolds into intelligence and movement, without ever losing the mark of its divine origin. The One, silent and ineffable, pours itself into the Intellect as an inexhaustible source of presence and truth; the Intellect, in contemplating itself and contemplating its source, generates the ordered plurality of the Forms; and the Soul, bearer of this fragmented light, imprints on the cosmos the vital breath that connects all things. This triad is not merely an abstract metaphysical structure, but the very expression of a vital dynamism, where each level of being preserves within itself the call to return and the impulse for reintegration into primal simplicity.

From this architecture arises a fundamental tension: each hypostasis carries within itself both the heritage of its origin and the need for expansion. The One, although absolutely transcendent, is not indifferent to what emanates from it — its fullness overflows precisely due to its excessive perfection. The Intellect, even inhabiting the sphere of pure contemplation, does not cease to also contemplate what derives from it, recognizing in the Soul the echo of its own intelligence.

And the Soul, in its incessant movement between the intelligible and the sensible, holds the dual impulse to give form to the world and to lead it, with all its imperfections, back to the first source of all being and all meaning.

In this journey, there is no rupture or essential loss: the sensible world, even if distant from the purity of the One, is not an absolute exile, but an intermediate landscape where the reflection of divine order still sparkles. One, Intellect, and Soul are, ultimately, expressions of the same process, the dynamic articulation of a unity that, without ever fragmenting, finds in its own emanation the path to its eternal reaffirmation. Therefore, understanding these hypostases is not only grasping a philosophical cosmology, but recognizing in the structure of being the same silent itinerary that every soul, one day, will be called to traverse.

Chapter 9
The Dynamics of Emanation

At the heart of the Neoplatonic worldview lies a fundamental dynamic that permeates all reality, from the primordial emanation of the One to the last vestige of manifest existence: the dynamic of procession and conversion, expressed in the Greek terms *proodos* and *epistrophe*. These two interconnected concepts describe the essential movement of reality, a continuous flow that departs from the divine source and unfolds towards multiplicity, and a movement of return, an innate longing that propels all creation back to its primordial origin. Understanding the dynamic of procession and conversion is crucial to grasping the Neoplatonic vision of the universe as an organic and hierarchical system, animated by an incessant cycle of distancing and rapprochement with the divine source, and to unveiling the path of the human soul in its ascetic and contemplative journey.

Procession (*proodos*) describes the movement of emanation of reality from the One, its gradual descent through the different levels of existence, from the intelligible world to the sensible world. This movement should not be understood as a creation *ex nihilo*, but rather as an unfolding, an expansion of divine reality from its primordial source. Procession is not an act of arbitrary will of the One, but rather a metaphysical necessity, a consequence of its superabundance and its intrinsic perfection. Just as a spring naturally overflows, the One, in its fullness, radiates reality outwards, without diminution or loss of its own essence. The emanations that proceed from the One are not separate or distinct from it, but rather gradual and differentiated manifestations of its primordial unity, expressions of its richness and its fecundity.

Procession follows a hierarchical order, descending from the most perfect and one to the less perfect and multiple. The One, in its absolute simplicity, emanates the Intellect, the domain of divine thought and Platonic Forms. The Intellect, in turn, emanates the Soul, the animating and organizing principle of the sensible world. The Soul, unfolding further, gives rise to the natural world, to the physical universe with its multiplicity of beings and phenomena. Each level of reality that emanates from the previous one preserves within itself the mark of its origin, but at the same time manifests a certain differentiation and complexification, resulting in a progressive decrease in perfection and unity as it distances itself from the One. This processional order is not rigid or linear, but rather organic and dynamic, allowing for a variety of intermediate levels and a complex interconnection between the different parts of reality.

Conversion (*epistrophe*), in turn, describes the movement of return of reality back to its primordial source, the innate longing that propels all creation back to the One. This movement is not a mere reversal of procession, but rather an internal impulse, a desire inscribed in the very nature of each being, to return to its origin and to realize its full potentiality. Conversion is the creation's response to the call of the One, a movement of love and desire that seeks union and reintegration into the divine source. Just as procession is a metaphysical necessity, conversion is an ontological longing, a search inherent in the nature of being.

Conversion manifests itself in different forms at different levels of reality. In the natural world, conversion is expressed through the cycles of nature, the movement of the stars, the growth of plants, the search for the preservation of life. In living beings, conversion manifests itself through the instinct of self-preservation, the desire for reproduction, the pursuit of pleasure and happiness. In the human soul, conversion manifests itself in a more conscious and explicit way, through the desire for knowledge, the search for truth, the aspiration to beauty and goodness, and, ultimately, the longing for union with the divine. The human soul, conscious of its divine origin and its exiled condition in the material world, feels a profound longing for the return to its spiritual homeland, for reintegration into the unity and perfection of the One.

The human soul plays a special role in the dynamic of conversion. Endowed with reason and free will, the human soul is capable of carrying out conversion consciously and deliberately, choosing the path of virtue, contemplation, and mystical union. Through the practice of philosophy, meditation, prayer, and ascetic purification, the human soul can free itself from the shackles of the body and the material world, rise above passions and sensible illusions, and turn towards the Intellect and the One in search of illumination and union. The ascetic and contemplative journey of the human soul is, therefore, the paradigm of conversion, the exemplary path that reveals the fundamental dynamic of Neoplatonic reality.

Ascetic practice, in the context of conversion, is not limited to a mere renunciation of sensible pleasures or a mortification of the body, but rather to a process of purification and transformation of the soul, aiming to make it fit to receive the divine light and to unite with the One. The soul needs to purify itself from disordered passions, material attachments, and sensible illusions that distance it from its divine origin and keep it bound to the world of multiplicity and change. This purification involves the cultivation of moral virtues, such as justice, temperance, courage, and wisdom, which harmonize the faculties of the soul and prepare it for intellectual contemplation. Ascetic practice also includes spiritual exercises, such as meditation, prayer, and contemplation of nature, which elevate the soul above discursive thought and open it to intellectual intuition and mystical experience.

Contemplation, in turn, is the apex of conversion, the moment in which the soul, purified and elevated, reaches union with the divine. Contemplation is not an act of discursive thought or conceptual analysis, but rather a direct and immediate intellectual intuition, a mystical experience that transcends reason and the senses. In contemplation, the soul unites with the Intellect and, ultimately, with the One itself, realizing its full spiritual potentiality and finding the peace, happiness, and plenitude it seeks. This mystical union is not a fusion or annihilation of individuality, but rather a participation in divine life, a communion with the One, a contemplation of its beauty and its perfection. Contemplation is the ultimate objective of the soul's journey, the culminating point of the dynamic of conversion.

Thus, the dynamic of emanation and return reveals itself as the essential pulse of the Neoplatonic cosmos, where each being, from the most minute particle to the conscious soul, participates in a cosmic cycle of distancing and reintegration. There is no absolute rupture or division between the levels of being, but a vibrant continuity, like a cosmic breath where the One exhales multiplicity and, at the same time, draws back everything that proceeds from it. This incessant flow is the very structure of reality, where being is only fully realized when it recognizes itself as part of this larger movement, when it understands that its ultimate destiny is not to remain in dispersion, but to rediscover itself in the primordial unity that always sustains it.

For the human soul, this dual movement takes on a particularly dramatic character. In its exile in the sensible world, the soul experiences the tension between the attraction to the mutable forms of matter and the silent call of intelligible eternity. It is in this intermediate space, between the visible and the invisible, that it is invited to choose—to follow the descending flow of multiplicity or to turn to the luminous source that generated it. Each desire for beauty, each search for meaning, each deep restlessness is an echo of this ancestral call, a fragmented memory of its divine origin that resonates in the very heart of its earthly existence.

And it is precisely in this conscious choice that the human soul finds its singular role in the cosmic drama of emanation and conversion. More than a passive piece in the universal order, the awakened soul is called to be a conscious reflection of the very movement of the cosmos, a living bridge between the sensible and the intelligible, between shadow and light. By purifying itself of illusions and ascending through knowledge and contemplation, it not only fulfills its individual destiny, but collaborates with the very dynamic of the universe, reintegrating multiplicity into unity and restoring in itself the lost harmony—a harmony that is, from the beginning, the echo of the inexhaustible simplicity of the One.

Chapter 10
The Cosmic Order and the Hypostases

The architecture of Neoplatonic reality is not limited to an abstract hierarchy of metaphysical principles, but unfolds and manifests itself in the cosmic order, in the concrete universe that we perceive and inhabit. For the Neoplatonists, the cosmos is not a chaotic set of random elements, but rather an ordered and intelligible system, structured according to the emanation of the hypostases and animated by the dynamics of procession and conversion. Understanding how the hypostases manifest themselves in the cosmic order implies unveiling the Neoplatonic vision of the universe as a living and hierarchical organism, traversed by a continuous current of divine reality, and perceiving the position of the human being within this vast and complex cosmic structure. The cosmic order is not only an objective datum, but also a mirror that reflects the divine order, a path for contemplation and for the soul's ascension towards its primordial source.

The cosmic order, from a Neoplatonic perspective, is intrinsically linked to the hierarchy of the hypostases. Each level of the cosmos corresponds to one or more hypostases, manifesting their characteristics and attributes in a specific way. The higher levels of the cosmos, closer to the One, reflect the unity, intelligence, and perfection of the primary hypostases, while the lower levels, further from the divine source, manifest the multiplicity, materiality, and change characteristic of the Soul and the sensible world. This correspondence between the cosmic levels and the hypostases is not a mere analogy, but rather an expression of the very ontological structure of reality, which unfolds and manifests itself in different degrees of perfection and complexity.

At the top of the cosmic order is the Intelligible World (κόσμος νοητός), the domain of purely intelligible reality, corresponding to the hypostases of the One and the Intellect. This world transcends space and time, change and materiality, constituting the realm of eternity and immutability. In the Intelligible World, the One resides, the primordial source of all reality, ineffable and unknowable, beyond all representation and all concept. Below the One, the Intellect manifests itself, the domain of divine thought and Platonic Forms, the seat of cosmic intelligence and absolute truth. The Intelligible World is the paradigm of perfection and unity, the ideal model according to which the sensible world is configured, the object of philosophical contemplation, and the ultimate destination of the soul's ascetic journey.

Below the Intelligible World is situated the Anima World (κόσμος ψυχικός), the domain of the World Soul and individual souls. This world constitutes the bridge between the intelligible and the sensible, participating in both domains and mediating their relationship. In the Anima World, the World Soul governs and animates the cosmos, ordering the celestial movements, distributing life and intelligence among living beings, and maintaining the harmony and cohesion of the universe. Individual souls, parts of the World Soul, inhabit this cosmic level before incarnating into material bodies, or return to it after death, in a continuous cycle of incarnation and discarnation. The Anima World is characterized by movement, change, and temporality, in contrast to the immutability and eternity of the Intelligible World, but still preserves a proximity to divine reality, manifesting its order, beauty, and intelligibility.

Finally, at the base of the cosmic order, is the Sensible World (κόσμος αἰσθητός), the material universe that we perceive through our senses, corresponding to the most external and differentiated manifestation of the Soul. This world is characterized by multiplicity, change, imperfection, and materiality, constituting the level of reality furthest from the One. In the Sensible World, natural phenomena, physical bodies, terrestrial living beings, and the totality of the material universe manifest themselves. Although distant from the perfection of the Intelligible World, the Sensible World is not devoid of divine presence, but rather an imperfect and transient reflection of the order and beauty that emanate from the higher hypostases. The Sensible World participates in the intelligibility of the Soul and the Intellect, manifesting an order and structure that can be known by human reason, and reveals, through its natural beauty and cosmic harmony, a vestige of the divine perfection that permeates all reality.

The influence of the hypostases extends through all levels of the cosmic order, shaping its structure, animating its life, and guiding its movement. The One, although transcendent and ineffable, radiates its unity and perfection to all levels of the cosmos, constituting the ultimate foundation of its existence and its order. The Intellect illuminates the cosmos with its divine intelligence, making it knowable and intelligible, and manifesting the Platonic Forms as ideal models for sensible reality. The Soul animates the cosmos with its vital force, conferring upon it movement, life, and order, and mediating the relationship between the intelligible world and the sensible world. This influence of the hypostases is not static or punctual, but rather dynamic and continuous, maintaining the cosmos in a state of constant flux, animated by the dynamics of procession and conversion.

The Neoplatonic vision of the cosmos as a hierarchical system emanated from the divine implies a specific understanding of the position of the human being within this cosmic order. The human being, constituted of body, soul, and intellect, participates in all levels of reality, being a microcosm that reflects the structure of the macrocosm. The human body belongs to the sensible world, sharing its materiality and transience. The human soul, essentially part of the World Soul, connects the human being with the anima world, conferring upon them life, sensitivity, and movement. The human intellect, in turn, participates in the divine

Intellect, enabling the human being to know the truth, to contemplate the Forms, and to aspire to union with the One. This complex and multifaceted nature of the human being places them in a unique position within the cosmic order, as a mediator between the sensible world and the intelligible world, capable of ascending to the contemplation of the divine and of realizing their full spiritual potentiality.

The contemplation of the cosmic order, from a Neoplatonic perspective, is not only an intellectual exercise, but also a spiritual path, a way for the soul's ascension towards the divine. By contemplating the beauty, order, and harmony of the cosmos, the human being can recognize the presence and action of the hypostases at different levels of reality, and awaken their innate desire for the return to their divine origin. The cosmic order thus becomes a mirror that reflects the divine order, an open book that reveals the wisdom and beauty of the Creator, a step in the ascetic journey of the soul towards mystical union. Neoplatonic philosophy, in this sense, is not only a theory about the cosmos, but also a spiritual practice, a way of life that aims to lead the human soul to its full realization, through the contemplation of the cosmic order and the ascension towards the higher hypostases.

The cosmic order, as described by the Neoplatonists, is not a simple external framework that delimits reality—it is, rather, the very living expression of the divine in its unfolding. Each layer of the cosmos, each plane of existence, not only points to the transcendent origin, but also resonates with its silent presence, like increasingly faint echoes of the primal plenitude. This presence does not impose itself abruptly or violently, but manifests itself in the gentleness of natural order, in the regularity of celestial movements, in the harmony of forms and proportions, as if the cosmos itself were an invisible scripture, in which primordial unity allows itself to be glimpsed amidst multiplicity.

It is in this ordered horizon that the human being finds their deepest vocation. By participating in all layers of reality, they are called to perceive, in their own being, the reflection of this universal structure. Their body, subject to the incessant flux of matter and time, still carries the animating breath of the World Soul; their soul, linked to the great cosmic soul, vibrates in tune with the universal order; and their intellect, a spark of the divine Intellect, holds the key to the contemplation of eternal truth. This interweaving is not accidental, but a calling: man, by understanding himself as a microcosm, also understands himself as a living bridge between earth and heaven, between the sensible and the intelligible.

To contemplate the cosmic order, therefore, is not only to admire the beauty of the external world, but to recognize oneself in it, to feel oneself part of a movement that transcends the individual and involves them in a greater flow of emanation and return. Each gaze cast at the harmony of the sky, each intuition of beauty in nature, is a discreet summons for the soul to resume its ascending journey. Thus, Neoplatonic philosophy offers not only a metaphysical map of reality; it proposes a reconciliation, a reunion between the cosmos and the soul, between knowledge and life, and between the human being and the originating light which, even hidden beneath layers of multiplicity and forgetfulness, never ceases to shine in its silent call.

Chapter 11
Primary Hypostases

The architecture of the primary hypostases – the One, the Intellect, and the Soul – constitutes the fundamental foundation of Neoplatonism, a conceptual structure that, despite its overall coherence, did not present itself as a monolithic and immutable dogma throughout the history of the school. On the contrary, Neoplatonic thought flourished through a continuous and dynamic dialogue, in which different philosophers interpreted, developed, and enriched the doctrine of primary hypostases, introducing nuances, variations, and complexities that reveal the richness and vitality of this philosophical current. Exploring the interpretations and variations in the primary hypostases among the main Neoplatonists – Plotinus, Porphyry, Proclus, and Iamblichus – allows us to unveil the evolution of the concept of hypostasis, the different emphases and perspectives adopted by each thinker, and the gradual complexification of the Neoplatonic system over the centuries.

Plotinus, considered the founder of Neoplatonism, established the foundations of the doctrine of primary hypostases in his *Enneads*, presenting an original and powerful vision of the One, the Intellect, and the Soul as the fundamental principles of reality. In Plotinus' philosophy, the One emerges as the primordial and transcendent source of all existence, radically simple, ineffable, and unknowable. The Intellect, emanating from the One, manifests itself as the domain of divine thought and Platonic Forms, the seat of cosmic intelligence. The Soul, in turn, emanates from the Intellect and turns towards the sensible world, animating the cosmos and mediating between the intelligible and the material. Plotinus' emphasis falls on the absolute transcendence of the One and on the journey of the individual soul towards mystical union with this primordial source. His presentation of the primary hypostases is characterized by a certain simplicity and conciseness, focusing on the essential aspects of each level of reality and its relationship with the supreme principle.

Porphyry, a disciple of Plotinus and responsible for the edition and organization of the *Enneads*, contributed significantly to the systematization and dissemination of Neoplatonism. In his works, Porphyry sought to clarify and organize the thought of his master, elaborating on the fundamental concepts and seeking to respond to objections and difficulties that might arise in the interpretation of the doctrine of the hypostases. Although he remains faithful to the general lines of Plotinian thought, Porphyry introduces some nuances and particular emphases, especially with regard to the psychology of the human soul and the path of virtue as preparation for contemplation. Porphyry's systematization facilitated the understanding and transmission of Neoplatonism to subsequent generations, making the Plotinian system more accessible and organized.

Proclus, the main figure of the Neoplatonic school of Athens in the 5th century AD, represents the apogee of the complexification and systematization of late Neoplatonism. In his vast and erudite works, Proclus developed an extremely elaborate and hierarchical metaphysical system, considerably expanding the doctrine of primary hypostases and introducing a myriad of intermediate levels of divine reality. Proclus did not limit himself to the One-Intellect-Soul triad, but multiplied the hypostases, interspersing between them a series of monads, dyads, and triads that fill the space between the One and the sensible world. His approach is characterized by extreme meticulousness and logical rigor, seeking to demonstrate the derivation of each level of reality from the previous one through complex and detailed arguments. In Proclus' philosophy, the Intellect unfolds into various intellectual hierarchies, and the Soul branches out into different levels of cosmic and particular souls, resulting in a metaphysical architecture of great complexity and sophistication. Proclus' elaboration reflects an attempt to account for the richness and diversity of manifest reality, as well as to respond to the difficulties and aporias that arose in the interpretation of the Plotinian system.

Iamblichus, a Neoplatonic philosopher of the 4th century AD, represents a different strand of late Neoplatonism, characterized by a greater emphasis on the theurgic and ritualistic aspects of philosophy.

Although he also accepts the doctrine of primary hypostases, Iamblichus integrates elements of Chaldean religion and magic into the Neoplatonic system, proposing a path of spiritual ascent that is not limited to intellectual contemplation, but that includes ritual and theurgic practices as means to achieve union with the divine. In Iamblichus' perspective, gods and demons play an important role in the cosmic hierarchy, interspersing between the primary hypostases and the sensible world, and theurgy, the art of invoking the gods through rituals and symbols, becomes a legitimate and effective path to spiritual elevation. Iamblichus' approach reflects a tendency of late Neoplatonism towards a greater integration of philosophy with religion and mysticism, seeking a path of salvation that involves not only reason, but also emotion, imagination, and ritual practice.

The differences in interpretation among these and other Neoplatonists reveal important nuances in the conceptions of primary hypostases. While Plotinus emphasizes the simplicity and transcendence of the One and the individual journey of the soul, Porphyry systematizes and clarifies the Plotinian system, Proclus complexifies and hierarchizes the doctrine of hypostases, and Iamblichus integrates theurgical and ritual elements into the Neoplatonic path. These variations do not invalidate the fundamental unity of Neoplatonism, but rather enrich and diversify its expression, revealing the capacity of this philosophical current to adapt and renew itself over time. The different emphases and perspectives adopted by each thinker reflect their specific philosophical and spiritual concerns, as well as the intellectual and cultural context in which they were inserted.

The evolution of the concept of hypostasis in late Neoplatonism, particularly with Proclus and Iamblichus, reflects a trend towards greater complexification and hierarchization of the system, as well as a greater integration of philosophy with religion and mysticism. Late Neoplatonism sought to respond to the difficulties and aporias that arose in the interpretation of the Plotinian system, elaborating on the intermediate levels of divine reality and seeking a path of salvation that involved not only reason, but also emotion, imagination, and ritual practice. This evolution should not be seen as a deviation or a degeneration of original Neoplatonism, but rather as a natural and legitimate development, an expression of the vitality and adaptability of this philosophical current.

In the unfolding of this philosophical tradition, the incessant movement between conceptual purification and metaphysical amplification reveals the very pulse of Neoplatonic thought, which never allowed itself to be enclosed in fixed schemes or dogmatic systems. Each interpretation, whether in the ascetic purification of Plotinus, the didactic ordering of Porphyry, the hierarchical architecture of Proclus, or the theurgic spirituality of Iamblichus, not only responds to specific philosophical and spiritual challenges, but also projects Neoplatonism beyond its immediate historical limits, allowing it to dialogue with mystical, theological, and philosophical traditions far beyond its time and place of origin.

This internal dynamism, where the search for the ultimate foundation of reality coexists with the need to explain the mediations and processes of return to the principle, confers on Neoplatonism a rare plasticity. The primary hypostases, far from being merely a static triad, become living landmarks of a speculative and spiritual journey, in which the cosmos, the soul, and divine intelligence are constantly revisited and reinterpreted in light of new contexts and new demands for meaning. Thus, the One remains as the unattainable, but always intuited, horizon, while the intermediate structures multiply to account for the complexity of the path that the soul must traverse.

In this sense, the history of the primary hypostases is also the history of a thought that refuses to divide philosophy and spirituality, reason and mystery. Each new interpretive layer added by the Neoplatonists, instead of obscuring the original simplicity of Plotinus, reveals the constant effort to articulate the ineffable within the horizon of language and human experience. This tension between the search for conceptual clarity and the preservation of mystery defines the singularity of Neoplatonism and guarantees its constant presence in the philosophical and spiritual dialogues that traverse centuries.

Chapter 12
The Legacy of the Hypostases

The impact of the primary hypostases of Neoplatonism – the One, the Intellect, and the Soul – transcended the boundaries of late antiquity, reverberating through the centuries and profoundly influencing Western philosophy and thought. From medieval and Renaissance philosophy to mysticism and theology, and even in contemporary resonances, the legacy of the primary hypostases manifests in diverse and multifaceted ways, attesting to the enduring relevance of Neoplatonic thought for our understanding of the divine, reality, and the journey of the human soul. Exploring this legacy implies tracing the invisible threads that connect Neoplatonism with later currents of Western thought, revealing the continuity and transformation of Neoplatonic ideas throughout history.

The influence of the hypostases on medieval philosophy is undeniable and profound. Neoplatonism, through the works of Plotinus, Porphyry, and Proclus, exerted a decisive impact on the development of Christian philosophy, especially in the Patristic period and in Scholasticism. Thinkers such as Augustine of Hippo, Pseudo-Dionysius the Areopagite, John Scotus Eriugena, and Albertus Magnus, among many others, incorporated and adapted Neoplatonic concepts, integrating them into Christian theology and metaphysics. The doctrine of the Trinity, in particular, was deeply influenced by the hierarchy of the hypostases, with the Father being associated with the One, the Son with the Intellect (Logos), and the Holy Spirit with the Soul or divine Love. The conception of God as transcendent and ineffable, but also immanent and present in the world, reflects the influence of Neoplatonic metaphysics. The emphasis on the soul's journey towards God, through purification, illumination, and mystical union, also largely derives from Neoplatonic soteriology. The philosophical and metaphysical vocabulary of Neoplatonism, such as the concepts of emanation, participation, hierarchy, and contemplation, became an integral part of the lexicon of medieval philosophy, shaping the language and structure of theological and philosophical thought of the time.

In Renaissance philosophy, Neoplatonism experienced a true renaissance, becoming one of the most important and influential philosophical currents of the period. Interest in Neoplatonism was driven by the rediscovery and translation of the works of Plato and Plotinus, as well as by the development of humanism and interest in classical culture. The Platonic Academy of Florence, founded by Marsilio Ficino under the patronage of Cosimo de' Medici, became a center for the study and dissemination of Neoplatonism, profoundly influencing Renaissance culture and thought. Ficino translated the complete works of Plato and Plotinus into Latin, making them accessible to a wider audience, and developed an original synthesis of Neoplatonism with Christianity, proposing a vision of the universe as a hierarchy of beings emanated from God and animated by a desire to return to their primordial source. Other Renaissance thinkers, such as Pico della Mirandola, Nicholas of Cusa, and Giordano Bruno, also drew inspiration from Neoplatonism, developing their own interpretations and adaptations of the primary hypostases and Neoplatonic cosmology. Renaissance philosophy, under the influence of Neoplatonism, was characterized by an emphasis on the value and dignity of the human soul, on its capacity to ascend to the contemplation of the divine and to realize its creative and spiritual potential.

Neoplatonism also left an indelible mark on Western mysticism, influencing both Christian mysticism and other mystical traditions. The soul's journey towards union with the divine, the concept of mystical ecstasy as an experience of direct and immediate contact with the transcendent, and the apophatic language used to describe the ineffable nature of God, are themes and motifs that Neoplatonism bequeathed to the Western mystical tradition. Christian mystics such as Meister Eckhart, John of the Cross, and Teresa of Ávila, among many others, used Neoplatonic language and concepts to describe their mystical experiences and to articulate their understanding of the relationship between the human soul and God. Neoplatonic mysticism, with its emphasis on transcendence, immanence, and the ascetic journey, offered a conceptual framework and an expressive language for mystical experience, profoundly influencing Western spirituality.

In theology, the legacy of the primary hypostases is also significantly felt. Christian theology, as already mentioned, incorporated and adapted Neoplatonic concepts from its beginnings, especially with regard to the doctrine of the Trinity and the understanding of divine nature. Negative theology, which seeks to approach God through the negation of all positive attributes, derives directly from the apophatic theology of Neoplatonism, which recognizes the ineffability and transcendence of the One. Mystical theology, in turn, is inspired by Neoplatonic soteriology, describing the soul's journey towards God as a process of purification, illumination, and union, culminating in the mystical experience of ecstasy and contemplation. Even in contemporary theology, Neoplatonism continues to be a source of inspiration and reflection, offering a vocabulary and a conceptual framework for thinking about the relationship between God and the world, divine transcendence and immanence, and the human search for meaning and transcendence.

In contemporary Western thought, the resonances of Neoplatonism and the primary hypostases can be found in various areas, from the philosophy of religion and spirituality to depth psychology and aesthetic theory. In the philosophy of religion, Neoplatonism continues to be studied and debated as one of the most important and influential philosophical traditions of late antiquity, offering a complex and sophisticated model for understanding the nature of the divine and the relationship between reason and faith. In contemporary spirituality, Neoplatonism inspires the search for a non-dogmatic and non-institutionalized spirituality, based on inner experience, contemplation of nature, and the quest for union with the transcendent. In depth psychology, especially in the archetypal psychology of Carl Jung and James Hillman, Neoplatonism is seen as a source of insights into the structure of the human psyche, the dynamics of the unconscious, and the journey of individuation. In aesthetic theory, the Neoplatonic concept of intelligible beauty and the emphasis on aesthetic contemplation as a path to spiritual elevation continue to resonate, influencing our understanding of art, beauty, and aesthetic experience.

The long reverberation of the primary hypostases through Western thought reveals how the triad of One, Intellect, and Soul did not remain merely a metaphysical construction enclosed in itself, but became a universal language to describe the fundamental tension between the absolute and the multiple, between transcendence and immanence, between the divine and the human. This conceptual plasticity allowed each era to project its own spiritual and philosophical concerns onto the Neoplatonic model, adapting it to its questions and demands. From the speculations of the Church Fathers to the dialogues between philosophy and mysticism, passing through the Renaissance ideal of man's ascent to the divine, the hypostases were continuously reinterpreted as a mirror and symbol of the most essential searches of the Western soul.

Throughout this trajectory, the very meaning of the hypostases expanded, transcending their original role as steps of being to also become metaphors of interiority, language, and symbolic creation. If in Plotinus the soul longed to return to its immaculate origin, in the mystical and existential currents that succeeded him, this return took on multiple contours: ethical purification, aesthetic intuition, amorous ecstasy, or intellectual illumination. Each unfolding of Neoplatonism was not merely a gesture of preservation, but a reinvention, in which the hypostases echoed as living figures of a journey where reason, contemplation, and mystery intertwine without ceasing.

Thus, more than a static legacy, the primary hypostases left as inheritance a method of thinking the ineffable, a grammar to express the unspeakable, and a constant invitation to surpass the limits of the visible and the sayable. In this incessant movement of appropriation and reinvention, Neoplatonism crosses history as a kind of underground current, nourishing reflections on the nature of being, the condition of the soul, and the possibility of touching, even if in glimpses, the lost unity that, even veiled, continues to pulsate in the heart of existence.

Chapter 13
Aeons, the Intermediate Beings

In the vast panorama of Neoplatonic cosmology, beyond the primary hypostases of the One, Intellect, and Soul, emerges a myriad of intermediate beings that populate the realms of divine reality, acting as links and differentiated manifestations of the fullness of being. Among these intermediate beings, the Aeons occupy a prominent place, especially in the development of late Neoplatonism and in Gnostic currents that share roots and influences with Neoplatonic thought. To begin the exploration of the universe of the Aeons, it becomes fundamental to introduce this complex concept, defining it in the Neoplatonic and Gnostic context, situating it in the hierarchy of divine reality, and elucidating its essential function as mediators between the primary hypostases and the manifest world. The understanding of the Aeons as intermediate beings opens a new horizon in our journey of knowledge of Neoplatonism, revealing the richness and diversity of divine reality and the intricate system of mediations that structures it.

The definition of Aeons in the Neoplatonic and Gnostic context requires a careful approach, considering the nuances and particularities of each system of thought. In Neoplatonism, the term Aeon (from the

Greek αἰών, aión, which means "era," "long duration," "eternity") acquires a specific philosophical and theological meaning, designating divine beings or entities that emanate from the Intellect or the Soul, situated at intermediate levels of the hierarchy of being. The Aeons are not primary hypostases, such as the One, the Intellect, and the Soul, but rather differentiated manifestations of these hypostases, expressions of their inner richness and their capacity to unfold into a multiplicity of forms and functions. In the Gnostic context, the term Aeon assumes even greater importance, becoming a central element of Gnostic cosmology and soteriology. In Gnostic systems, the Aeons are understood as emanations of the Unknowable Father, constituting the Divine Plenitude (Pleroma), the realm of light and perfection that opposes the material world, considered as a domain of darkness and ignorance. Although there are significant differences between the Neoplatonic and Gnostic conceptions of the Aeons, both traditions agree in attributing to these intermediate beings a crucial role in the mediation between the transcendent divine and the manifest world.

In the Neoplatonic system, the Aeons are understood as emanations of the Intellect and the Soul, deriving their existence and characteristics from the primary hypostases. While the Intellect represents the domain of pure thought and Platonic Forms, the Aeons manifest a certain differentiation and particularization within this domain, personifying specific divine qualities, such as Wisdom, Love, Justice, Beauty, Truth, and many others. The Aeons can be understood as "living ideas" or "divine intelligences" that emanate from the Intellect, revealing its richness and its inner fecundity. Likewise, the Aeons can also be considered as emanations of the Soul, expressions of its capacity to animate and order the cosmos at different levels of reality. In this case, the Aeons manifest the action of the Soul in the world, distributing life, order, and intelligence throughout the different domains of creation. The emanation of the Aeons from the Intellect and the Soul does not imply a diminution or degeneration of divine reality, but rather an expansion and diversification of its manifestation, an expression of its infinite richness and potentiality.

The main function of the Aeons, both in Neoplatonism and in Gnosticism, is that of mediators between the primary hypostases and the manifest world. Situated at intermediate levels of the hierarchy of being, the Aeons act as links between the transcendent divine and created reality, facilitating communication, influence, and interaction between the different levels of existence. The Aeons make the divine more accessible and comprehensible to finite creatures, manifesting divine qualities and attributes in a more concrete and particularized way. They also serve as guides and helpers on the soul's journey towards the divine, guiding and assisting it in its search for mystical union. The mediating function of the Aeons is essential for the economy of divine reality, ensuring the order and harmony of the cosmos and facilitating communication between the Creator and creation.

As intermediate beings, the Aeons occupy an ambiguous and paradoxical position in the hierarchy of being. On the one hand, they belong to the divine domain, participating in the perfection and eternity of the primary hypostases. On the other hand, they turn to the manifest world, taking interest in its order, its life, and its destiny. This dual orientation of the Aeons reflects their mediating nature, their function as a bridge between the transcendent and the immanent, the eternal and the temporal, the one and the multiple. The Aeons are border beings, situated on the threshold between the divine and the human, sharing characteristics of both domains and acting as intermediaries between them. Their ambiguous and paradoxical nature makes them fascinating and complex figures, capable of revealing the richness and diversity of divine reality in all its dimensions.

This constitutive ambiguity of the Aeons, which positions them between immutable eternity and the dynamic flow of creation, confers upon them a vibrant and almost dramatic character within Neoplatonic and Gnostic cosmology. They are not merely passive reflections of the primary hypostases, but active agents in the distribution of order and meaning throughout the extent of the cosmos. Each Aeon carries within itself a spark of divine Intelligence, while at the same time responding to the need for plurality and differentiation inherent in manifest reality. This role makes them essential not only for the ontological sustenance of the world, but also for the very possibility of knowledge and spiritual ascension, since it is through them that the soul recognizes, in each degree of existence, the echo of a superior perfection.

Beyond their metaphysical functions, the Aeons also serve as symbolic figures, condensing in their presences qualities, tensions, and archetypes that reflect both the divine order and the dilemmas of the human soul. Their plurality is not a mere excess or a gratuitous multiplication of entities, but the expression of the very internal fertility of the Intellect and the Soul, which can only manifest their plenitude through this richness of forms, names, and attributes. Each Aeon, therefore, not only illuminates a face of divine reality, but also reflects the spiritual possibilities of the soul in its quest to return to the One, mirroring virtues, states of consciousness, and stages of the inner path.

In this sense, the Aeons are not just distant cosmic entities, but active presences in the drama of spiritual ascension. They constitute the living language with which the divine makes itself known, the symbolic and ontological fabric that sustains the soul's return to its source. By mediating between the transcendent and the immanent, they weave a bridge that does not annul the distance between the Creator and creation, but makes it habitable, transforming each degree of existence into an invitation to contemplation and conscious participation in the mystery of being. It is in this incessant dialogue between the Aeons and the pilgrim soul that the cosmos reveals itself not only as an ordered space, but as a spiritual itinerary, where each step is a response to the call of eternity.

Chapter 14
Divine Plenitude

Within the conceptual universe that involves the Aeons, emerges the Pleroma, a term of Greek origin that resonates with meanings of plenitude, totality, and divine completeness. The Pleroma, in the context of both late Neoplatonism and, even more prominently, in Gnosticism, is configured as the transcendent realm of the Aeons, the space of divine plenitude where these intermediary beings manifest the richness and diversity of supreme reality. Exploring the structure of the Pleroma implies entering the hierarchical organization of the Aeons within this transcendent domain, unveiling the relationships of interdependence and emanation that connect them, and understanding the essential connection of the Pleroma with the primary hypostases, particularly with the Intellect, from which the Aeons emanate. Immersing oneself in the structure of the Pleroma reveals the complexity and sophistication of the cosmology that involves the Aeons, illuminating their function as differentiated manifestations of divine plenitude and steps on the soul's journey towards its transcendent origin.

The Pleroma, derived from the Greek πλήρωμα (pleroma), literally means "fullness," "completeness," "abundance." In the philosophical and religious context, the term acquires a technical connotation, referring to the transcendent realm of divinity, the space of divine plenitude where the Aeons and other spiritual entities reside. The Pleroma is the domain of light, perfection, and immortality, as opposed to the material world, often conceived as a realm of darkness, imperfection, and transience, particularly in Gnostic currents. In late Neoplatonism, and especially in Gnosticism, the Pleroma is presented as a complex hierarchical structure, organized into different levels or orders of Aeons, each manifesting a specific divine quality and performing a particular function within the economy of reality. The Pleroma is not a physical or spatially delimited space, but rather a metaphysical reality, a state of being characterized by divine plenitude and perfection.

The hierarchical organization of the Aeons within the Pleroma reflects the order and harmony that permeate divine reality, even in its differentiated manifestation. Within the Pleroma, the Aeons do not appear as an indistinct mass of divine beings, but rather as an organized and interconnected structure, in which each Aeon occupies a specific place and performs a particular function in relation to the others. The hierarchy of the Aeons in the Pleroma can be understood as a progression of perfection and power, starting from the Aeons closest to the primordial source and descending towards the frontier with the manifest world. The higher Aeons, situated closer to the Intellect, manifest divine qualities in a purer and more intense form, while the lower Aeons, further from the source, express these qualities in a more differentiated and particularized way, preparing the way for the manifestation of reality in the sensible world. This hierarchy does not imply an inequality or an intrinsic inferiority of some Aeons in relation to others, but rather a functional diversity and a distribution of tasks within the economy of divine plenitude. Each Aeon, regardless of its hierarchical position, contributes essentially to the harmony and completeness of the Pleroma, manifesting a particular facet of the richness and diversity of divine reality.

The relationship of the Pleroma with the primary hypostases, and especially with the Intellect, is one of emanation and dependence. The Pleroma, as the realm of the Aeons, emanates from the Intellect, the second primary hypostasis, in the same way that the Intellect emanates from the One. The Intellect, as the domain of divine thought and Platonic Forms, constitutes the primordial source from which the Aeons derive their existence and their characteristics. The Aeons can be understood as unfoldings or specifications of the Intellect, differentiated manifestations of its thought and intelligence. The Pleroma, therefore, is not separate or independent from the Intellect, but rather an extension or an expansion of its reality, a development of its inner richness and its capacity to manifest itself in a multiplicity of forms. The relationship between the Pleroma and the Intellect is comparable to the relationship between a tree and its fruits: the fruits emanate from the tree, manifesting its life and its fecundity, but remain intrinsically linked to their origin, depending on the sap and vitality of the tree for their own existence. The Pleroma, as the realm of the Aeons, depends on the Intellect as its primordial source, and manifests its richness and diversity as expressions of divine intelligence and fecundity.

The structure of the Pleroma, with its hierarchical organization of Aeons emanated from the Intellect, reflects the complexity and sophistication of Neoplatonic and Gnostic cosmology. This structure is not merely an abstract scheme or a theoretical construction, but rather an attempt to account for the richness and diversity of divine reality, to explain the multiplicity of manifestations of the divine in the world, and to trace a map of the soul's journey towards its transcendent origin. The Pleroma, as the realm of the Aeons, offers a space of mediation between the ineffable One and the manifest world, allowing divine reality to become more accessible and comprehensible to finite creatures. The Aeons, within the Pleroma, act as intermediaries, as steps that facilitate the soul's ascent towards the divine, guiding and assisting it in its search for mystical union. The structure of the Pleroma, therefore, is not only a cosmological element, but also a soteriological aspect, related to the path of salvation and illumination of the human soul.

If the Pleroma represents the absolute plenitude of divinity, it is in it that the tension between unity and multiplicity that runs through all Neoplatonic and Gnostic thought becomes visible. Each Aeon, while expressing a specific quality or attribute of the Intellect, preserves within itself the mark of the One, as if each fragment of plenitude carried in its essence the memory of original simplicity. In this way, the Pleroma is not a chaotic dispersion of divine entities, but a harmonious orchestration in which each Aeon sings its own note, contributing to the cosmic symphony of divine self-manifestation. This ordered totality makes the Pleroma not only the space where the Aeons reside, but the very living expression of divinity in its incessant unfolding.

However, the Pleroma is not only a mirror of divine perfection; it is also the invisible bridge that connects the ineffable One to the sensible and mutable cosmos. Along this chain of emanations, the Aeons, as links between the higher and lower planes, veil and reveal the primordial light. They make the divine partially intelligible without ever exhausting its mystery, offering the pilgrim soul images, symbols, and presences that allow it to intuit, albeit in a fragmented way, the greater reality of which it is a part. Therefore, the Pleroma is simultaneously a reflection of eternity and an invitation to the spiritual crossing, where each Aeon is a door and each divine quality, a calling.

In the soul's journey of return to its principle, the Pleroma reveals itself as a map and a promise. As the soul traverses the spheres of the Aeons, it recognizes in each of them not only a cosmic dimension, but a forgotten aspect of itself. The ascension, therefore, is not only a cosmic crossing, but an inner reconciliation, where knowing the Pleroma is rediscovering oneself with one's own luminous origin. Thus, the Pleroma is not only the abode of divine beings, but the very landscape of primordial memory, where the soul, exiled in time and matter, rediscovers the vastness of its true home.

Chapter 15
Time and Eternity

In the intricate system of Neoplatonic and Gnostic thought, the relationship between the Aeons and the notions of time and eternity reveals itself as a complex and profoundly significant theme. The Aeons, as intermediary beings who inhabit the Pleroma or Divine Fullness, not only fill the space between the transcendent divine and the manifest world, but also stand on the threshold between eternity and time, participating in both dimensions and mediating their interaction. Unveiling the relationship between the Aeons and the manifestation of time and eternity implies exploring the temporal and atemporal nature of these divine beings, understanding how they influence our perception of time in the material world, and perceiving how the contemplation of the Aeons can lead us to an experience of eternity. Immersing oneself in this theme reveals the Neoplatonic and Gnostic view of time not as a mere linear succession of moments, but as a manifestation of eternity, a river that flows from the timeless ocean of divinity.

The nature of the Aeons, concerning time and eternity, is fundamentally paradoxical and ambiguous, reflecting their intermediate position in the hierarchy of being. On one hand, the Aeons participate in divine eternity, inhabiting the Pleroma, which is described as a timeless and immutable realm, beyond the vicissitudes of time and change. From this perspective, the Aeons can be considered as eternal beings, sharing in the immortal and incorruptible nature of divinity. Their existence is not subject to temporal duration, the succession of instants, or the flow of time, but rather to the permanence and stability of the eternal present. In this sense, the contemplation of the Aeons can be understood as a way to transcend time and participate in divine eternity, an anticipation of the eternal bliss that awaits the soul after its liberation from the body and the material world.

On the other hand, the Aeons also manifest a certain temporal dimension, especially in their mediating function and in their relationship with the manifest world. Although they inhabit the eternal realm of the Pleroma, the Aeons turn towards the temporal world, taking interest in its destiny and influencing its course. From this perspective, the Aeons can be considered as "temporal" beings in the sense that their activity manifests in time, exerting an influence on the events and temporal processes that occur in the material world. Their mediation between the divine and the world implies a certain descent or projection of eternity into time, a temporal manifestation of the atemporal reality of the Pleroma. In this sense, the Aeons can be seen as the "lords of time," the regents of the cosmic cycles and temporal rhythms that govern the manifest universe.

The temporal and atemporal nature of the Aeons reflects the very ambiguity of the concept of time in Neoplatonism and Gnosticism. Time is not simply denied or devalued in these traditions, but rather understood in relation to eternity, as a manifestation or an imperfect and transient image of atemporal reality. Time, from this perspective, is not just a linear succession of moments, but a cycle, a rhythm, a cosmic dance that reflects the order and harmony of eternity. Eternity, in turn, is not merely the absence of time, but the fullness of being, the totality of divine reality that transcends temporal and spatial limitations. Time and eternity are not, therefore, separate and opposing realities, but interconnected and interdependent dimensions, in which time manifests eternity in a veiled and transient way, and eternity reveals itself in time through its rhythms and cycles.

The influence of the Aeons on the perception of time in the material world is significant and multifaceted. The Aeons, as intermediary beings between eternity and time, act as filters or mediators through which eternity manifests in the temporal world. Our perception of time, consequently, is conditioned by the influence of the Aeons, who shape our temporal experience and allow us to glimpse, albeit fleetingly and indirectly, the atemporal reality of divinity. The regularity of natural cycles, the succession of seasons, the rhythm of day and night, the movement of celestial bodies—all of this can be interpreted as manifestations of the influence of the Aeons in the temporal world, as expressions of the eternal order and harmony that are reflected in the flow of time. The very human experience of time, with its subjective dimension and its relationship to consciousness and memory, can also be understood in light of the influence of the Aeons, who shape our perception of the past, present, and future, and open us to the possibility of transcending the linearity of time and experiencing moments of eternity in time.

The contemplation of the Aeons, in this context, can become a path to the experience of eternity, a way of accessing the atemporal realm of divinity. By contemplating the Aeons, in their divine qualities and cosmic manifestations, the human soul can rise above the limitations of time and space, transcend the succession of moments and temporal attachments, and glimpse the eternal reality that underlies the flow of time. Meditation on the Aeons, the invocation of their divine qualities, the contemplation of their beauty and harmony, can lead the soul to a state of ecstasy and mystical union, in which the experience of time dissolves into the timelessness of eternity. In this sense, the Aeons act as steps not only in the hierarchy of being, but also in the temporal journey of the soul, guiding it through time towards eternity, and facilitating its ascension to the atemporal realm of divinity.

In this subtle dialogue between time and eternity, the Aeons appear as liminal presences, guardians of the threshold where the perpetual fragments into instants and the flow of time attempts to recall its motionless origin. Each Aeon, in manifesting a divine quality within the cosmos, imprints on the fabric of time a reflection of eternity—as if each cycle, each natural or spiritual rhythm, echoed the memory of what always is, even when clothed in the transience of the now. Therefore, time, in the Neoplatonic and Gnostic horizon, is not a complete exile from eternity, but a veiled reverberation of it, a ciphered invitation for the soul, in deciphering the secret pulse of the world, to remember the primordial stillness from whence it came.

The mediating function of the Aeons does not consist only in leading the soul to the vertical return to the One, but in teaching it to see eternity hidden in the furrows of time. It is not only by fleeing time that eternity is glimpsed—it is also by penetrating its mystery and understanding that each instant, however ephemeral, contains a vestige of the eternal. The Aeons, as architects of cosmic rhythm, mark the beat of this invisible dance, in which linear time and sacred time intertwine, offering the attentive soul portals for the direct contemplation of divine fullness.

Thus, the soul's journey through time is not a mere passage through an empty corridor towards eternity, but a secret school where each experience, each cycle, and each partial revelation can prepare the spirit to recognize, under the mask of change, the immutable face of the divine. In this journey, the Aeons are simultaneously masters and companions—voices that guide, lights that attract, and mirrors in which the soul, in contemplating the eternal order, rediscovers that time is, in its most secret core, the moving remembrance of lost eternity.

Chapter 16
Divine Qualities

In the intricate panorama of the Pleroma, the Aeons do not manifest as undifferentiated entities, but rather as living and radiant personifications of divine qualities, radiating the richness and diversity of the supreme nature. Each Aeon, within the Divine Plenitude, embodies a specific virtue or attribute of the divine, such as Wisdom, Love, Strength, Beauty, Justice, Peace, Joy, among many others. Exploring the relationship between the Aeons and the divine qualities implies delving into the universe of theological virtues as conceived in Neoplatonism and Gnosticism, understanding how each Aeon personifies a specific quality, revealing the variety and richness of these divine qualities, and perceiving how the contemplation of the Aeons can become a path to communion with these virtues and to the spiritual development of the human soul. Immersion in this theme reveals the Aeons not merely as intermediary beings, but as mirrors that reflect the multiple facets of divine perfection, inviting the soul to harmonize with these qualities and to realize its own virtuous nature.

Each Aeon, in the Pleroma, is understood as a personification of a specific divine quality, a living and conscious manifestation of a particular attribute of divinity. This personification is not limited to a mere symbolic or allegorical representation, but rather a real and ontological incarnation. Each Aeon is the divine quality itself in act, its full and perfect expression in the realm of Divine Plenitude. Thus, for example, an Aeon may personify Divine Wisdom, being Wisdom itself in its essence and most elevated manifestation. Another Aeon may personify Divine Love, being Love itself in its primordial source and in its most intense irradiation. And so on, each Aeon embodying a specific virtue or attribute of the divine, revealing a particular facet of its perfection and richness.

The variety and richness of the divine qualities manifested by the Aeons reflect the infinite complexity and superabundance of the divine nature. The divine is not limited to a single quality or attribute, but manifests in a multiplicity of virtues and perfections, each expressing a particular aspect of its essence and action. The Aeons, as personifications of these divine qualities, reveal the diversity and richness of the divine, showing that divine perfection is not monolithic or reducible to a single attribute, but rather a symphony of virtues and perfections that harmonize and complement each other. Among the divine qualities personified by the Aeons, we find Wisdom (Sophia), Love (Agape), Strength (Dynamis), Beauty (Kallos), Justice (Dikaiosyne), Peace (Eirene), Joy (Chara), Immortality (Athnasia), Life (Zoe), Truth (Aletheia), and many others. This list is not exhaustive, and different Neoplatonic and Gnostic systems may present variations in the nomenclature and organization of the Aeons and their divine qualities. The important thing is to perceive that the diversity of Aeons and divine qualities reflects the infinite richness and complexity of the divine nature, which transcends any attempt at reduction or simplification.

The contemplation of the Aeons can become a path for us to connect with these divine qualities and to cultivate them in our own souls. By directing our attention and our meditation to the Aeons, by contemplating their divine qualities and by invoking their presence, we can open ourselves to the influence of these virtues and allow them to penetrate and transform our consciousness. The contemplation of the Aeon of Wisdom, for example, can awaken in us the desire for true knowledge and for a deep understanding of reality. The contemplation of the Aeon of Love can expand our capacity to love unconditionally and to connect with others on a deeper level. The contemplation of the Aeon of Strength can instill in us courage and resilience to face life's challenges and to persevere on the spiritual path. And so on, each Aeon offering a portal to a specific divine quality, a path to its realization and manifestation in our own lives.

The connection with divine qualities through the contemplation of the Aeons is not just an intellectual or imaginative exercise, but a transformative spiritual practice, capable of producing real and lasting effects in our soul. By opening ourselves to the influence of divine qualities, we allow them to purify and illuminate our consciousness, harmonize our inner faculties, and bring us closer to our own divine nature. The cultivation of theological virtues, such as wisdom, love, and strength, is not just an ethical or moral ideal, but an ontological necessity, an essential requirement for the realization of our full spiritual potential and for union with the divine. The contemplation of the Aeons, in this sense, becomes a practical path for inner transformation and spiritual development, a way of accessing the sources of virtue and perfection that reside in the heart of divinity.

The richness and variety of the divine qualities manifested by the Aeons invite the soul on a journey of discovery and exploration, a path through the multiple gardens of divine virtue. Each Aeon offers a new perspective on the nature of the divine, revealing a particular aspect of its perfection and beauty. The contemplation of the totality of the Aeons and their divine qualities can lead the soul to a broader and deeper understanding of the divine nature, to a synoptic vision of the plenitude and harmony of the Pleroma. This synoptic vision, in turn, can awaken in the soul an even more intense desire for union with the divine, a deep longing for participation in the life and beatitude of the Divine Plenitude.

The soul's journey through the Pleroma, as it encounters this myriad of divine qualities embodied in the Aeons, reveals itself as a slow and progressive attunement to the very essence of the divine. Each virtue contemplated and assimilated imprints on the spirit a subtle reflection of the primordial light, making the soul not just a spectator, but a living participant in the great chorus of perfections that sustain cosmic harmony. In this silent dance between contemplator and contemplated, the soul is called to recognize in itself the echo of these eternal qualities, which lie dormant within it like seeds waiting for the touch of light to blossom in fullness.

The recognition of each Aeon as a living and conscious emanation of a divine quality does not lead to a fragmentation of the vision of the divine, but, paradoxically, to the perception of the unity that permeates everything. The Love of the Pleroma is not opposed to Wisdom, just as Strength does not negate Peace; on the contrary, each quality exists in intimate interdependence, sustaining and enriching the other in a tapestry that can only be fully understood by the spiritual gaze attuned to the vision of totality. In this way, the soul that walks the virtual paths of the Aeons is not content to collect virtues as isolated pieces, but strives to interweave them into its own being, until its interiority resonates with the same harmony that governs the Plenitude.

At the end of this contemplative and transformative journey, the soul no longer distinguishes between the divine and the human in its depths, for the divine qualities, once projected as distant realities in the Aeons, become the living pillars of its own spiritual structure. Wisdom, Love, Justice, and Beauty cease to be mere celestial attributes and become its own essential fibers, weaving into its being a garment of light capable of transiting without veils between worlds. And thus, the soul awakens to the understanding that, from the beginning, its destiny was not just to know the divine qualities, but to become one with them, a shimmering mirror of the luminous infinity that, from always, called it back to the heart of the Pleroma.

Chapter 17
Aeons and Archangels

As we explore the universe of intermediary beings in Neoplatonic cosmology and related spiritual traditions, the figure of Archangels emerges, a celestial hierarchy widely recognized in Judeo-Christian traditions and other religious currents. The relationship between Aeons and Archangels invites a fascinating comparative analysis, seeking to identify the parallels and distinctions between these two categories of intermediary beings, unraveling their mediating functions, hierarchical position, and connection with the divine. Investigating Aeons in relation to Archangels implies drawing bridges between Hellenistic philosophical thought and the religious traditions of the Middle East, revealing possible mutual influences and conceptual convergences, and expanding our understanding of the role of intermediary beings in the economy of divine reality. The comparative analysis between Aeons and Archangels enriches our perspective on both categories, allowing us to grasp their specific characteristics and their relevance to the spiritual journey of the human soul.

To begin the comparative analysis between Aeons and Archangels, it is crucial to define each category within its respective context. We have already explored Aeons as emanations of the Intellect and the Soul in Neoplatonism, personifications of divine qualities that inhabit the Pleroma and act as mediators between the transcendent divine and the manifest world. Archangels, in turn, emerge from Judeo-Christian traditions as hierarchically organized celestial beings, messengers of God, executors of His will, and protectors of humanity. In the Judeo-Christian celestial hierarchy, Archangels are situated at a level superior to common Angels, but inferior to other higher hierarchies, such as Seraphim and Cherubim, forming an intermediate order between the divine and the human. Although the origins and contexts of Aeons and Archangels are distinct, their mediating function and their hierarchical position within a system of divine reality present notable parallels that deserve to be explored.

One of the most evident parallels between Aeons and Archangels lies in their mediating function. Both Aeons and Archangels act as intermediaries between the transcendent divine and the manifest world, facilitating communication and interaction between these two domains. Aeons, as we have seen, mediate between the Pleroma and the sensible world, transmitting divine qualities and influencing the cosmic order. Archangels, similarly, act as messengers of God, transmitting His word and His will to human beings, and as agents of divine providence, executing His plans and intervening in the world in His name. Both, Aeons and Archangels, serve as bridges between heaven and earth, between the divine and the human, making the transcendent more accessible and comprehensible to finite creatures. This mediating function is essential for the economy of divine reality in both traditions, ensuring communication and harmony between the different levels of existence.

Another point of convergence between Aeons and Archangels lies in their hierarchical position within a system of divine reality. In both Neoplatonism and Judeo-Christian traditions, intermediary beings are organized in complex hierarchies, reflecting the order and harmony that permeate the divine universe. Aeons, in the Pleroma, are organized into different levels and orders, reflecting the progressive differentiation of divine reality as it emanates from the Intellect. Archangels, in a similar manner, occupy a specific position in the Judeo-Christian celestial hierarchy, forming one of the nine angelic orders, each with its particular functions and attributes. This hierarchical organization suggests a vision of the divine universe as an ordered and well-structured system, in which each intermediary being plays a specific role and contributes to the harmony of the whole. Both the hierarchy of Aeons and the hierarchy of Archangels reflect the complexity and richness of divine reality, and their organization into different levels and orders suggests a progressive differentiation and specialization of mediating functions.

Despite the evident parallels, there are also important distinctions between Aeons and Archangels, reflecting their distinct origins and cultural and religious contexts. One of the most notable distinctions lies in their conceptual origin. Aeons emerge from a Hellenistic philosophical context, deriving from the metaphysical speculations of Neoplatonism and Gnosticism, while Archangels originate from Judeo-Christian religious traditions, based on biblical scriptures and rabbinic and patristic theology. This difference in origin is reflected in their specific characteristics and attributes, as well as in their function and role within the system of divine reality. Aeons, in their philosophical origin, tend to be conceived in a more abstract and metaphysical way, as personifications of divine qualities or as cosmic intelligences, while Archangels, in their religious origin, tend to be conceived in a more personal and anthropomorphic way, as messengers of God and protectors of humanity.

Another important distinction lies in their specific functions. Although both act as mediators, their mediating functions manifest in different ways. Aeons, in Neoplatonism, focus more on cosmological mediation, influencing the order of the universe and transmitting divine qualities to the manifest world, while Archangels, in Judeo-Christian traditions, focus more on soteriological and revelatory mediation, guiding humanity on the path of salvation and transmitting divine revelations. This difference in emphasis reflects the different concerns and objectives of the Neoplatonic and Judeo-Christian traditions: Neoplatonism, with its emphasis on the soul's ascent and mystical union, focuses more on cosmological mediation and the contemplation of divine qualities, while Judeo-Christian traditions, with their emphasis on a personal relationship with God and the salvation of the soul, focus more on revelatory mediation and divine action in human history.

Despite the distinctions, it is possible to find points of convergence and dialogue between the conceptions of Aeons and Archangels. Some late Neoplatonic thinkers, influenced by the religious currents of their time, sought to integrate elements of Judeo-Christian traditions into the Neoplatonic system, identifying Aeons with angelic hierarchies or establishing parallels between the divine qualities personified by Aeons and the attributes of God in biblical scriptures. Similarly, some Christian theologians, influenced by Neoplatonic philosophy, used Neoplatonic concepts to interpret and elaborate on the doctrine of Archangels, understanding them as manifestations of divine intelligence and will and as links between God and creation. This dialogue and interaction between Neoplatonic and Judeo-Christian traditions reveal the universal human search for understanding divine reality and the role of intermediary beings in mediation between the transcendent and the immanent.

The relationship between Aeons and Archangels, when observed through the lens of an integrating cosmology, suggests that philosophical and spiritual traditions, even starting from distinct points of origin, share a common intuition: the need to recognize in the fabric of divine reality presences that not only reflect the light of the supreme principle, but make it accessible and active in the sensible world. Whether as expressions of eternal attributes or as messengers invested with a historical and personal mission, Aeons and Archangels respond to the same longing to create bridges between the incomprehensible and the human, between the absolute and the concrete experience of the soul. It is in this space of mediation that the divine gradually reveals itself, allowing finite consciousness to glimpse, step by step, the vastness of transcendent fullness.

In this transit between heaven and earth, the metaphysical qualities of Aeons and the revelatory function of Archangels seem to intertwine as two complementary aspects of the same quest: to translate mystery into language, eternity into movement, and essence into presence. The traditions that gave rise to them, even if marked by worldviews and distinct spiritual objectives, end up witnessing the same certainty — that the divine never isolates itself in its inaccessibility, but constantly extends its emanations or its messengers to touch, guide, and awaken the human to the memory of its celestial origin. By walking the paths traced by Aeons and Archangels, the soul is called to recognize itself as heir and recipient of this incessant communication between worlds.

Thus, by exploring the intersections and divergences between these intermediary figures, we not only broaden our understanding of the traditions that shaped them, but also discover the echo of a spiritual inquietude that crosses cultures and centuries: the desire to understand how the divine bends towards the world, without losing its transcendence, and how the human is called to rise to respond to this call. Aeons and Archangels, each in their own way, guard and sustain this fragile and essential bridge between the realms, keeping alive the hope that, at some point in the crossing, light and word become one truth within the awakened soul.

Chapter 18
The Philosophy of Plotinus

In the dawn of Neoplatonism, the seminal figure of Plotinus rises as the original architect of a philosophical system that would profoundly influence Western thought. Although the nomenclature and systematization of hypostases and Aeons became more explicit and complex with his successors, it is in Plotinus, in his Enneads, that we find the seeds and conceptual foundations for understanding intermediate beings and the hierarchy of divine reality.

Immersion in Plotinus' philosophy reveals an original and nuanced vision of intermediate beings, where the emphasis falls on the richness and diversity of the Divine Intelligence itself, rather than on a rigid hierarchy of separate entities.

To understand Plotinus' approach to Aeons, it is crucial to situate it within the general context of his philosophy and cosmology. Plotinus established a hierarchical emanationist system, where reality flows from the One, the primordial and transcendent source of all existence, through a descending progression of hypostases. After the One, emanates the Intellect (Nous), the domain of divine thought, the realm of Platonic Forms, and the first manifestation of multiplicity from primordial unity. From the Intellect, in turn, emanates the Soul (Psyché), the animating principle of the cosmos, which mediates between the intelligible world and the sensible world, ordering and vitalizing material reality. This fundamental hypostatic triad – One, Intellect, and Soul – constitutes the backbone of Plotinian cosmology, describing the flow of divine reality and its progressive differentiation.

It is important to note that in Plotinus' work, we do not find an explicit and systematic elaboration of the concept of Aeons in the same way that we will see in later Neoplatonists such as Iamblichus or Proclus, or in Gnostic currents. Plotinus does not extensively use the term "Aeon" (Aion in Greek) to designate a specific category of intermediate beings in the hierarchy of being. However, this does not mean that the idea or concept of divine intermediate beings or levels is absent from his philosophy. On the contrary, when analyzing the Enneads, we realize that Plotinus, although he does not use later nomenclature, presents elements and ideas that can be interpreted as precursors to the concept of Aeons, or as implicit ways of understanding mediation and diversity within divine reality.

Where, then, can we find the "implicit Aeons" in Plotinus' philosophy? The answer lies mainly in the Intellect (Nous). Plotinus describes the Intellect as a domain of unimaginable richness and diversity, the place of Platonic Forms, divine thought in its fullness. Within the Intellect, there is not a monotonous unity, but rather an ordered multiplicity, a cosmic dance of intelligences and forms that contemplate each other and radiate towards the lower world. It is within this diversity and differentiation of the Intellect that we can identify proto-Aeonic elements in Plotinian philosophy.

In the Enneads, Plotinus describes the Intellect not as a monolithic block of thought, but as a living and dynamic realm, full of "intellectual lives" and "divine intelligences." These "divine intelligences" can be interpreted as differentiated manifestations or aspects of the Intellect itself, particular expressions of its thought and activity. Although Plotinus does not explicitly name them "Aeons," these intellectual entities play a mediating role, transmitting the light of the Intellect to the lower levels of reality and personifying specific divine qualities, very similarly to the function attributed to Aeons in later Neoplatonic systems.

An elucidative example can be found in Plotinus' description of Platonic Forms. The Forms, residing in the Intellect, are not mere static archetypes, but rather living and intelligent entities, endowed with power and influence over the sensible world. Each Form, such as the archetype of Beauty, Justice, or Wisdom, can be understood as a particular manifestation of divine intelligence, a divine quality personified and radiated from the Intellect. In this perspective, Platonic Forms, within Plotinus' Intellect, can be seen as proto-Aeons, prefiguring the later idea of divine entities personifying specific qualities.

Another way to understand the "implicit Aeons" in Plotinus is through his description of the activity and "energy" of the Intellect. Plotinus emphasizes that the Intellect is not passive or static, but dynamic and radiant, overflowing in activity and divine energy. This "energy" of the Intellect can be interpreted as manifesting itself in various currents or flows of divine intelligence, each personifying a particular aspect of the Nous' thought. These "flows of divine intelligence," emanating from the Intellect and acting as intermediaries between the intelligible and the sensible world, approach the mediating function attributed to Aeons in later systems. The energy of the Intellect, in this reading, manifests itself in a differentiated way, giving rise to a multiplicity of divine entities or forces that act as intermediaries, although Plotinus does not explicitly classify them as "Aeons."

It is important to emphasize that Plotinus' approach to intermediate beings, implicit in the concept of the Intellect, differs from the later systematization of Aeons. Plotinus does not establish a complex hierarchy of Aeons between the Intellect and the Soul, as Iamblichus or Proclus will do. For Plotinus, the main hierarchical differentiation lies in the three primary hypostases – One, Intellect, and Soul – and the multiplicity of divine intermediate beings is found primarily within the domain of the Intellect. In Plotinus, the emphasis falls on the unity and simplicity of the Intellect, despite its inner richness and diversity, and not on the creation of a new hierarchical layer of separate entities between the Intellect and the Soul.

In contrast to the later development of the concept of Aeons in late Neoplatonism, where Aeons become increasingly personalized and independent entities, Plotinus' approach maintains a more intimate and immediate connection between intermediate beings and the Intellect as their primordial source. Plotinus' "implicit Aeons" are best understood as aspects or manifestations of Divine Intelligence itself, expressions of its inner richness and its capacity to manifest itself in a diversified way. They are less hierarchically distinct entities and more facets of the same precious gem of the Divine Intellect.

A careful reading of the Enneads reveals that, for Plotinus, divine multiplicity never implies fragmentation or distancing from the originating principle. Even the subtlest differentiations within the Intellect are but modes of manifestation of a single and same intelligible light, which, as it expands, preserves in each ray the memory of the primordial radiance. In this incessant movement of self-recognition and irradiation, the Intellect unfolds without ever departing from itself, and it is in this unfolding that one can glimpse the genesis of intermediate beings, not as autonomous or hierarchically prominent entities, but as the very internal rhythms of divine consciousness in its fullness.

This intrinsic character of Plotinian emanations, in which each form of intelligence or each expression of beauty and virtue cannot be isolated from its originating whole, marks a subtle but fundamental difference in relation to the later conception of more personalized and hierarchized Aeons. In Plotinus, emanations do not crystallize into rigid entities, but remain malleable and transparent, immediate reflections of divine thought in its own act of thinking itself. This fluidity ensures that mediation between worlds is not perceived as a static bridge between distant spheres, but as a continuous vibration of divine presence at all levels of reality.

Thus, Plotinus' philosophy anticipates and inspires the later development of the doctrine of Aeons, but preserves a delicate economy of unity and diversity, in which intermediate forms are not external steps or mediators between insurmountable distances, but expressions of the very intimacy of the divine being. It is in this integrated vision that Plotinus invites us to contemplate the invisible hierarchy that links the One to the sensible world — not as a ladder of separations, but as a living current of luminous intelligences, flowing from the heart of the One and returning to the contemplative soul the certainty that all that is multiple, in its deepest root, is but a variation of primordial unity.

Chapter 19
Other Neoplatonists

If Plotinus sowed the seeds of the concept of Aeons in Neoplatonism, albeit in a more implicit way and focused on the Intellect, it was his successors, notably Iamblichus and Proclus, who cultivated and expanded this idea, transforming it into a central and complex element of late Neoplatonic cosmology. These philosophers, operating in a different historical and intellectual context, sought to systematize and hierarchize divine reality more explicitly, attributing to the Aeons a prominent role as intermediate levels between the primary hypostases and the manifested world. Immersing oneself in the thought of Iamblichus and Proclus demonstrates the evolution of late Neoplatonism towards an increasingly elaborate systematization and hierarchization of divine reality, where the Aeons become essential steps in the soul's journey and vivid manifestations of divine plenitude.

Iamblichus, a Neoplatonic philosopher of the 4th century AD, represents an important transition in the development of the concept of Aeons. While maintaining the basic structure of Plotinian cosmology, Iamblichus introduces a greater emphasis on hierarchy, mediation, and the theurgic aspects of Neoplatonic philosophy. Regarding the Aeons, Iamblichus begins to delineate a more explicit categorization and a more complex hierarchy than we find in Plotinus. While Plotinus concentrated multiplicity and differentiation within the Intellect, Iamblichus begins to distinguish and name intermediate entities between the Intellect and the Soul, moving closer to the Gnostic conception of a Pleroma inhabited by a host of divine beings.

In Iamblichus' philosophy, the Aeons begin to be seen as more personalized and independent entities, endowed with names, specific functions, and defined places in the cosmic hierarchy. Iamblichus not only recognizes the existence of the Aeons but also dedicates himself to classifying and organizing them into complex hierarchies, drawing inspiration partly from Chaldean and Egyptian religious traditions, in addition to Neoplatonic sources. In his works, Iamblichus describes different orders of Aeons, associating them with specific divine qualities, planetary and cosmic divinities, and different levels of intelligible and psychic reality. This categorization and hierarchization of the Aeons by Iamblichus represents a significant development in relation to Plotinus, where divine multiplicity, previously more contained within the Intellect, begins to expand and manifest more explicitly through a hierarchy of intermediate beings.

Proclus, leader of the Neoplatonic Academy of Athens in the 5th century AD, takes the complexification and systematization of the concept of Aeons to an even greater level. In his vast and erudite work, Proclus develops an extremely elaborate and hierarchical metaphysical system, considerably expanding the doctrine of hypostases and introducing a myriad of intermediate levels of divine reality. Proclus not only welcomes and expands the categorization of the Aeons initiated by Iamblichus but also integrates this Aeonic hierarchy into an even more complex and detailed metaphysical system, interposing it between the primary hypostases and the manifested world.

In Proclus' cosmology, the Aeons occupy a central and prominent place. He not only multiplies the orders of Aeons but also organizes them into intricate and ramified hierarchies, interposing them between the Intellect and the Soul, and subdividing them into different classes, families, and triads. Proclus elaborates on the emanation of the Aeons from the Intellect, detailing the processes by which the unity of the Nous unfolds into Aeonic multiplicity, and describing the relationships of interdependence and participation between the different levels of the Aeonic hierarchy. The complexity of the Aeonic hierarchy in Proclus reflects an attempt to account for the infinite richness and diversity of divine reality, to map all levels and nuances of the manifestation of the divine, and to fill all the empty spaces in the hierarchy of being.

One of the most characteristic aspects of Proclus' approach to the Aeons is their organization into triads and hexads. Inspired by Pythagorean mathematics and Chaldean theology, Proclus structures the Aeonic hierarchy in sets of triads and hexads, each corresponding to a specific level of divine reality and manifesting a particular combination of divine qualities and attributes. These triads and hexads are not mere abstract categories but real metaphysical entities, endowed with intelligence, power, and influence over the manifested world. The numerical and geometric complexity of the Aeonic hierarchy in Proclus reflects a search for order, harmony, and intelligibility in the description of divine reality, attempting to map the totality of being through mathematical and symbolic structures.

For Proclus, the Aeons are not just abstract hierarchical levels, but living and conscious beings, endowed with will, intelligence, and love. He describes the Aeons as "intellectual gods" or "secondary divinities", subordinate to the Intellect, but superior to the Soul and the sensible world. These Aeonic gods act as regents and governors of different domains of divine and cosmic reality, distributing the influence of the Intellect to the lower levels of being and ensuring the order and harmony of the universe. The personalization of the Aeons by Proclus, attributing to them almost anthropomorphic qualities and governmental functions, represents a significant departure from Plotinus' more abstract and metaphysical approach, moving closer to religious and mythological conceptions of intermediate divinities.

The complexification of Neoplatonic cosmology through the Aeons in Iamblichus and Proclus reflects a shift of emphasis within late Neoplatonism. While early Neoplatonism, represented by Plotinus, focused more on the unity and transcendence of the One, and on the individual soul's journey towards mystical union, late

Neoplatonism, with Iamblichus and Proclus, shifts the emphasis to hierarchy, mediation, and the complexity of divine reality. The interest turns to the detailed and systematized description of the cosmic order, to the elaboration of intricate hierarchies of intermediate beings, and to the integration of theurgic and ritual elements into philosophical practice. This shift in emphasis does not signify an abandonment of the fundamental principles of Neoplatonism, but rather an expansion and a diversification of its expression, an attempt to account for the richness and complexity of divine reality in a more meticulous and detailed way.

In contrast to the relative simplicity of Plotinian cosmology, late Neoplatonic cosmology, with Iamblichus and Proclus, becomes extremely complex and hierarchical, through the proliferation of intermediate levels and the elaboration of the Aeonic hierarchy. This complexification reflects a search for exhaustiveness and completeness in the description of divine reality, an attempt to map all the nooks and crannies of being, and to answer all the questions and difficulties that arose in the interpretation of the Plotinian system. The Aeonic hierarchy, in this context, becomes a fundamental instrument for the systematization and organization of divine reality, allowing late Neoplatonists to construct metaphysical systems of great breadth and sophistication.

In following this transition from early Neoplatonism to its late formulations, one perceives that the proliferation of Aeons and the increasing complexity of intermediate hierarchies do not emerge from a mere speculative or ornamental desire. Rather, they reflect a genuine attempt to articulate the experience of a cosmos saturated with divine presence, where each level of reality, each intelligence, and each virtue actively participates in the eternal movement that links the One to the sensible world. This meticulously interwoven web of emanations and returns does not merely describe an external order but serves as an inner map for the soul seeking to understand its own place in the cosmic order and in the incessant flow of divine manifestation.

If in Plotinus the flows of the Intellect still preserved the transparency of a unified field, in Iamblichus and Proclus each emanation gains more defined contours, as if the divine, in unfolding into its multiple aspects, was being clothed in names, faces, and functions. What is revealed, however, is not a loss of unity, but the recognition that the One communicates fully in diversity, and that the contemplation of the divine requires this loving attention to its multiple faces. To know the cosmos becomes, for the late Neoplatonists, to know the invisible links that sustain the continuity between the original light and the vibrant fabric of existence.

In this sense, the development of the concept of Aeons in the systems of Iamblichus and Proclus is not just a metaphysical or theurgic speculation, but a response to the spiritual need to map the way back to the divine, step by step, name by name. Each Aeon named, each triad unfolded, each intermediate intelligence carefully described represents an invitation to the soul to recognize itself as part of this vast divine community, where each fragment of light, however distant it may seem, holds within itself the memory of the One and the promise of return to its source.

Chapter 20
The Ascent of the Soul

In the intricate and ascending path of the human soul towards its divine source, the Aeons manifest themselves as more than mere inhabitants of a distant celestial realm; they are configured as essential steps, luminous and progressive stages that the soul must traverse to achieve mystical union with the Divine. The ascetic journey of the soul, in Neoplatonism, is not an abrupt leap into the transcendent, but rather a gradual and ordered ascent, a progression through increasingly subtle and perfect levels of reality, in which the Aeons play the crucial role of bridges and guides. Understanding the Aeons as steps to the Divine illuminates the progressive and hierarchical nature of the Neoplatonic spiritual journey, revealing a structured and assisted path to the realization of mystical union.

In the Neoplatonic view, the ascent of the soul is not a linear and homogeneous movement, but rather a progression through well-defined steps or stages, each marked by overcoming a lower level of reality and conquering a higher level. The Aeons, with their intermediate nature and their hierarchical position between the Intellect and the Soul, are configured as these progressive steps in the ascetic journey. Each

Aeon, personifying a specific divine quality, represents a particular stage of spiritual development, a step to be reached on the ladder of ascent. By ascending through the Aeonic hierarchy, the soul not only approaches the Divine, but also transforms itself inwardly, assimilating the divine qualities personified by each Aeon and purifying itself from the imperfections and limitations of its lower nature.

Each Aeon, with its specific divine quality, offers the soul a particular lesson and challenge on its ascetic path. The Aeon of Wisdom (Sophia), for example, represents the step of the search for true knowledge, of intellectual illumination, and of deep understanding of divine reality. To ascend this step, the soul must abandon the illusions of ignorance, cultivate a thirst for truth, and purify the mind of prejudices and unfounded opinions. The Aeon of Love (Agape), in turn, represents the step of union and compassion, of the expansion of the heart beyond selfishness and separation, and of experiencing unconditional love as the unifying principle of reality. The soul, to ascend this step, must purify its affections, free itself from possessive attachment, and cultivate benevolence and compassion for all beings. The Aeon of Strength (Dynamis) represents the step of will and determination, of overcoming obstacles and persevering on the spiritual journey. The soul, to reach this step, must strengthen its will, cultivate the courage to face challenges, and remain steadfast in the purpose of its divine quest. And so on, each Aeon offering a specific step in the ascent, with its particular lessons and challenges, leading the soul to a progressive and integral transformation.

Contemplation and invocation of the Aeons become, in this context, essential ascetic practices for progression on the spiritual journey. By contemplating a specific Aeon, the soul directs its attention and energy to the divine quality that it personifies, seeking to assimilate this virtue and integrate it into its own nature. Contemplation is not just a mental exercise, but a process of resonance and identification, in which the soul attunes itself to the vibration and energy of the Aeon, allowing its light to illuminate and transform it. Invocation, in turn, aims to attract the presence and help of the Aeon, asking for its guidance and power to overcome the challenges of the corresponding ascetic step. The combination of contemplation and invocation becomes a powerful method for progression on the spiritual journey, facilitating the ascent of the soul through the Aeonic steps and preparing it for union with the Divine.

The Aeons, in their function as steps to union, not only represent stages to be overcome, but also manifest themselves as benevolent guides and facilitators on the soul's journey. They are not obstacles to be overcome, but rather celestial allies that assist the soul at each stage of its ascent, offering guidance, protection, and strength. By initiating contemplation of an Aeon, the soul is not alone, but assisted by the presence and energy of that divine being, who inspires, encourages, and empowers it to progress on the ascetic path. The Aeons act as spiritual mentors, revealing to the soul the lessons and challenges of each step, showing it the virtues to be cultivated and the obstacles to be overcome, and offering it the necessary help to advance towards the Divine. The soul's journey, assisted by the Aeons, becomes not just an individual effort, but a cosmic collaboration, a dance between the aspirant and their celestial guides, a joint quest for union with the primordial source.

The ascent through the Aeonic steps culminates, finally, in union with the Divine, the ultimate goal of the soul's journey in Neoplatonism. By traversing the hierarchy of the Aeons, assimilating their divine qualities and purifying itself of its imperfections, the soul approaches ever closer to the primordial source of all reality, the transcendent and ineffable One. Progression through the Aeons is not just a hierarchical ascent, but also a process of interiorization and unification, in which the soul reconnects with its own divine nature and merges with the fullness of Being. Union with the Divine, in Neoplatonism, is not understood as an absorption or an annihilation of the soul's individuality, but rather as a harmonization and a perfect concordance with the will and nature of the One, an experience of its own innate divinity in full consciousness and realization. The Aeons, as steps to union, lead the soul to this state of beatitude and fullness, guiding it through the ascetic journey and preparing it for the mystical experience of divine union.

The ascending journey of the soul, accompanied and sustained by the silent presence of the Aeons, reveals that Neoplatonic asceticism is not just an effort of purification or an abstract itinerary of self-knowledge. It is, rather, an art of attunement and listening, in which each step reached corresponds to the opening of a new inner resonance, a fine adjustment between the movement of the soul and the pulsation of the divine cosmos. The Aeons, with their virtues and challenges, teach that spiritual ascent is not a linear achievement, but a continuous learning of harmony, where the soul, little by little, relearns to vibrate in the same tone as the higher spheres.

As the soul advances and recognizes itself in the divine qualities it has contemplated and assimilated, the Aeons cease to be external and distant figures to become mirrors of its own spiritual essence. Each virtue blossomed, each shadow dissolved, each layer of ignorance that gives way to light reveals that the path, although populated by guides and divine emanations, is also a return to the original truth that has always inhabited the soul. Thus, ascent is not an escape from the world or a denial of individuality, but a conscious reintegration of the soul into the universal rhythm, in which being and knowing, loving and understanding, become expressions of the same harmony.

And when, finally, the soul touches the threshold of the Ineffable, there is no longer separation between the step and the walker, between the Aeons and the light that animates them, between the search and the fullness found. The ascetic path unfolds in contemplative silence, where the One, without form and without name, welcomes the soul that, upon crossing the veils of the hierarchy, rediscovers itself as a pure reflection of the same primordial light. The role of the Aeons, fulfilled in each step of the climb, dissolves in that instant of recognition, where there are no masters or disciples left, only the eternal and ever-renewed reunion between the soul and its divine origin.

Chapter 21
Invocation of the Aeons

In the soul's journey towards union with the Divine, after understanding the Aeons as essential steps and benevolent guides, the next crucial step lies in exploring practical methods that allow us to establish a conscious and transformative connection with these intermediary beings. The contemplation and invocation of the Aeons are not mere intellectual exercises, but rather dynamic and living practices, capable of opening portals to divine reality and integrating Aeonic qualities and virtues into our daily experience. Diligent and intentional practice of contemplation and invocation thus becomes a powerful vehicle for spiritual transformation, opening the soul to the beneficial and illuminating influence of celestial beings.

One of the most accessible and effective methods to begin the contemplation of the Aeons is through guided meditation and creative visualization. This technique uses the power of imagination and mental concentration to create an inner space of stillness and receptivity, conducive to encountering the Aeons. In the practice of guided meditation, we can draw upon evocative descriptions of the celestial realms, divine qualities, and the symbolic characteristics of each Aeon.

We can, for example, visualize the radiant light of the Aeon of Wisdom, feel the loving energy of the Aeon of Love, or connect with the strength and determination of the Aeon of Strength. Creative visualization complements guided meditation, allowing the imagination to flow freely, opening space for spontaneous insights and unique personal experiences. During meditation, we can imagine ourselves ascending through the celestial realms, encountering the Aeons in their luminous domains, dialoguing with them, and absorbing their divine qualities. It is important to create a tranquil and comfortable environment, use soft music or nature sounds, and allow the mind to gradually quiet down, focusing attention on the visualization and the intention to connect with the chosen Aeon. Regular practice of this technique strengthens the capacity for concentration, sharpens intuition, and facilitates the perception of the subtle presence of the Aeons.

Another powerful approach to the contemplation of the Aeons lies in meditation with mantras and chants. Mantras, sacred syllables or phrases repeated rhythmically, can serve as vibrational tools to attune the mind to the energy and frequency of a specific Aeon. Different spiritual traditions associate mantras with specific divine qualities, and we can adapt or create mantras that resonate with the virtue we wish to contemplate in a particular Aeon. The repetition of the mantra, combined with mental concentration and visualization of the corresponding Aeon, can create a resonant energy field, facilitating connection and communication. Similarly, chants and hymns dedicated to divine qualities or celestial beings can be used as forms of invocation and contemplation. The sonic vibration of mantras and chants, combined with intention and devotion, elevates consciousness and opens channels of communication with the spiritual realms, allowing the soul to become attuned to the presence and influence of the Aeons.

Contemplative prayer and formal invocation represent more structured and directed methods for establishing a conscious dialogue with the Aeons. Contemplative prayer, in this context, goes beyond petition or supplication, becoming an expression of love, gratitude, adoration, and communion with the Divine through the Aeons. We can structure prayers that recognize the greatness and beauty of the Aeons, that express our desire to learn from their wisdom and to integrate their virtues into our lives, and that ask for their guidance and assistance on the spiritual journey. Formal invocation may involve the creation of simple rituals, using symbols, incense, candles, and other objects that resonate with the qualities of the Aeon being invoked. We can create altars dedicated to specific Aeons, where we can perform our practices of contemplation and invocation. It is important to emphasize that the main focus of invocation is not on manipulation or control of external forces, but rather on expressing our sincere intention of connection and communion, on opening the heart and mind to the beneficial influence of the Aeons, and on cultivating a relationship of respect and reverence with these celestial beings.

Beyond meditative practices and formal rituals, the contemplation of the Aeons can be integrated naturally and spontaneously into daily life, through the observation of nature and the appreciation of the arts. The contemplation of nature offers a mirror of cosmic order and beauty, revealing divine qualities manifested in the sensible world. By observing a sunset, the vastness of the ocean, the majesty of a mountain, or the delicacy of a flower, we can feel the presence and influence of the Aeons, recognizing their qualities personified in the beauty and harmony of the natural world. The appreciation of the arts, in its various forms of expression, can also become a vehicle for the contemplation of the Aeons. Music, painting, sculpture, poetry, and dance can express divine qualities such as beauty, harmony, truth, and love, allowing the soul to resonate with the energy of the Aeons through aesthetic experience. Integrating the contemplation of nature and the arts into daily life means cultivating a contemplative and sensitive gaze towards the world around us, recognizing the presence of the divine in all things, and opening the heart to the beauty and harmony that permeate creation.

It is fundamental, when beginning the practices of contemplation and invocation of the Aeons, to cultivate pure intention, discernment, and respect. Intention must be genuine and focused on spiritual growth, on the search for union with the Divine, and on the integration of divine qualities into our lives, and not on selfish goals or the pursuit of powers or material benefits. Discernment is essential to distinguish authentic experiences of spiritual connection from mere projections of the imagination or from misleading influences. Respect, finally, should guide our approach to the Aeons, recognizing their superior nature and approaching them with humility and reverence. The practice of contemplation and invocation of the Aeons should always be accompanied by an ethic of virtue and of action in the world, seeking to manifest divine qualities in our daily lives, in our relationships, and in our actions in the world, making ourselves instruments of divine light and goodness.

With the continuity of these practices and gradual immersion in sincere contemplation, the seeker begins to perceive that the Aeons are not just distant presences or archetypal symbols, but living forces that respond to the inner call of the soul. Their virtues do not remain isolated on the spiritual plane, but intertwine with the challenges, choices, and learnings of daily life, creating a golden thread that unites the visible world to the invisible. Each invocation therefore becomes a silent dialogue, in which the soul learns to listen to and recognize the subtle language of light, while the Aeons, with patience and compassion, teach the art of existing in communion with the divine in all circumstances of life.

Over time, this constant communion transforms the very perception of reality. The sacred ceases to be a separate instance, confined to moments of prayer or meditation, and begins to permeate every gesture, thought, and encounter. The contemplative gaze matures, capable of glimpsing the loving action of the

Aeons in the dance of daily events, in the cycles of nature, and even in the shadows that challenge the soul's growth. Connection becomes a state of spiritual presence, an inner listening attuned to the silent wisdom that guides the path back to the Center, where the Divine dwells in full unity with all things.

Thus, the call of the Aeons reveals itself not as an invitation to flee the world, but to immerse oneself in it with new awareness and reverence. Each invocation, each contemplation, and each silent response from the luminous realms are steps towards the recognition that the human being itself is a living reflection of these divine virtues. The spiritual journey, led by the invisible hand of the Aeons, becomes the art of remembering and restoring this forgotten spark, until soul and divine, invoker and invoked, contemplate each other as one.

Chapter 22
Critiques and Challenges to the Understanding of Aeons

The journey through the universe of Aeons, although fascinating and enriching, is not without obstacles and difficulties. The concept of Aeons, with its abstract nature, its origin in complex systems of thought, and its varied interpretation throughout history, has always represented a challenge to understanding, both for scholars of Neoplatonism and for those approaching this topic for the first time.

The critical analysis of difficulties and challenges does not aim to diminish the relevance or value of the study of Aeons, but rather to refine our understanding, making it more nuanced and aware of its complexities and ambiguities. By confronting criticisms and challenges, we strengthen our ability to interpret and apply the concept of Aeons in a more informed and insightful way.

One of the first and most evident difficulties in understanding Aeons lies in their own abstract and metaphysical nature. Aeons are not physical or concrete entities, capable of empirical observation or sensory definition. They belong to the domain of the intelligible, to the realm of pure thought and transcendent realities, which makes them inherently difficult to grasp by the discursive mind and conceptual language. The description of Aeons in Neoplatonic and Gnostic texts frequently resorts to symbolic, metaphorical, and allegorical language, which, although enriching and evocative, can also obscure their literal understanding and generate diverse and sometimes contradictory interpretations. The difficulty in translating the symbolic language of ancient texts into modern conceptual language represents a constant challenge for scholars and for those seeking to understand Aeons through contemporary lenses.

Another interpretative difficulty arises from the variety of conceptions of Aeons present in different currents of Neoplatonism and Gnosticism. As we explored in previous chapters, Plotinus' approach to Aeons is more implicit and focused on the Intellect, while Iamblichus and Proclus elaborate more complex and systematized Aeonic hierarchies. Gnostic currents, in turn, present an Aeonic Pleroma with characteristics and functions distinct from Neoplatonism. This diversity of perspectives and terminologies can generate confusion and hinder the apprehension of a unified and coherent concept of Aeons. The lack of a single and universally accepted definition of Aeons requires from the scholar a constant effort of contextualization and comparison between different sources and traditions, in order to discern the similarities, differences, and nuances of each approach.

Beyond the interpretative difficulties inherent in the nature of the concept and the variety of sources, the study of Aeons also faces criticisms and objections of a philosophical and theological nature. From the point of view of strict rationalism, the concept of Aeons can be dismissed as mere metaphysical speculation, devoid of empirical foundation and scientific validity. Rationalist critics may question the need to postulate invisible and unknowable intermediary entities to explain reality, advocating a more empiricist and materialist approach to understanding the world. The absence of direct empirical evidence for the existence of Aeons represents a challenge for those seeking rational and scientific validation for this concept.

From the point of view of some monotheistic theological traditions, the concept of Aeons can be seen as problematic for potentially compromising the absolute uniqueness and transcendence of God. Theological critics may argue that the proliferation of intermediary divine beings, such as Aeons, may dilute the primordial divinity and bring Neoplatonism closer to a polytheistic system, in contradiction with the monotheistic emphasis on the unity and singularity of God. The question of the compatibility between Neoplatonism and monotheism has been the subject of debates and controversies throughout history, and the conception of Aeons frequently occupies a central place in this discussion. The need to reconcile the Aeonic hierarchy with the transcendence and unity of the One represents a theological challenge for those seeking to integrate Neoplatonic thought with their monotheistic convictions.

In the realm of contemporary philosophy, the concept of Aeons can be questioned from various perspectives. Philosophical currents such as logical empiricism, positivism, and materialism tend to reject Neoplatonic metaphysics as unfounded speculation without relevance to understanding the real world. Contemporary philosophers may question the internal coherence of the Neoplatonic system, the validity of its metaphysical premises, and the relevance of the concept of Aeons to the problems and challenges of the contemporary world. The distance between the metaphysical language of Neoplatonism and the analytical and scientific language of contemporary philosophy represents an obstacle to communication and dialogue between these different traditions of thought.

Despite these criticisms and challenges, it is important to emphasize that the concept of Aeons continues to be the object of interest and debate in the academic and philosophical fields. Scholars of Neoplatonism are dedicated to analyzing and interpreting the different conceptions of Aeons present in ancient sources, seeking to clarify their ambiguities, resolve their contradictions, and understand their meaning within the Neoplatonic system. Contemporary philosophers, interested in metaphysics, philosophy of religion, and history of ideas, explore the relevance of the concept of Aeons for the understanding of consciousness, spiritual reality, and the human search for meaning and transcendence. Academic and philosophical debates about Aeons reflect the complexity and richness of this concept, and its capacity to raise profound questions and reflections even in the context of contemporary thought.

It is crucial, when approaching the concept of Aeons, to be aware of its difficulties and challenges, and to avoid an excessively literal or simplistic interpretation. The symbolic and metaphorical language of ancient texts requires an attentive and contextualized reading, which takes into account the nuances and ambiguities of Neoplatonic and Gnostic thought. Philosophical and theological criticisms must be faced with rigor and intellectual openness, recognizing the limitations and perspectives of each approach, and seeking a constructive dialogue between different traditions of thought. The understanding of Aeons should not be seen as a dogma or a blind belief, but rather as an invitation to exploration, reflection, and contemplation, an opportunity to expand our consciousness and to deepen our understanding of divine reality in all its dimensions.

Awareness of these criticisms should not be seen as an insurmountable obstacle, but as an essential part of the intellectual and spiritual journey that the study of Aeons provides. Confronting the difficulties inherent in their understanding allows not only to refine our reading, but also to cultivate an epistemological humility in the face of mysteries that surpass the limits of discursive reason. After all, the existence of Aeons — or even the possibility of their existence — invites us to recognize that reality is always vaster than the contours of language and human thought can encompass, being the very effort to understand them a form of training of the soul in the art of sustaining paradox and welcoming the ineffable.

At the same time, it is in the friction between tradition and criticism that the opportunity arises to update the concept of Aeons, freeing it from the shackles of a hermetic past and making it fertile for new dialogues with contemporary philosophy, science, and spirituality. The distance between Neoplatonic and Gnostic systems and current thought, far from being a barrier, can be a field of creation, where intuitions about the existence of mediating intelligences, divine archetypes, or invisible structures of the cosmos are reformulated and reinterpreted in the light of new sensibilities and knowledge. In this sense, Aeons do not need to be just conceptual relics of a lost world, but clues to a broader understanding of reality, capable of integrating both the visible and the invisible, the immanent and the transcendent.

Ultimately, the richness of the concept of Aeons perhaps lies precisely in its refusal to be imprisoned by rigid definitions or easy consensus. Its vocation is to inhabit the borders — between myth and philosophy, between mysticism and metaphysics — challenging each generation of seekers to find in it the reflection of their own spiritual anxieties. Whether as ontological realities, symbolic images, or instruments of contemplation, Aeons continue to remind us that the understanding of the divine, far from being a definitive conquest, is an infinite journey, where each step reveals not only new horizons, but also the vastness of all that we do not yet know how to name.

Chapter 23
Mythical and Poetic Imagination

In the realm of human understanding, where discursive reason sometimes encounters the limits of the inexplicable and the transcendent, mythical and poetic imagination emerges as an alternative and powerful path to apprehend subtle and complex realities. The concept of Aeons, with its abstract and metaphysical nature, resonates particularly with the symbolic and evocative language of myth and poetry, finding in these forms of expression a fertile ground for its manifestation and comprehension. Immersion in the relationship between Aeons and mythical and poetic imagination reveals a more intuitive and experiential dimension of spiritual knowledge, where beauty, emotion, and imagination become valid and enriching paths to understanding the Divine.

The appeal of the Aeons to mythical imagination lies in their very nature as archetypal and symbolic entities. The Aeons, personifications of divine qualities and levels of transcendent reality, do not present themselves as abstract and lifeless concepts, but rather as living and dynamic cosmic figures, full of meaning and evocative power. The language of myth, with its ability to personify forces of nature, to create cosmic narratives, and to express profound truths through symbols and allegories, finds in the Aeons a vast and rich field for its expression. Aeonic myths, present in Gnostic traditions and in certain branches of late Neoplatonism, describe the origin, hierarchy, functions, and interrelationships of the Aeons through symbolic and imaginative narratives that appeal to intuition and emotion more than to discursive reason. These myths should not be interpreted as literal historical accounts, but rather as symbolic expressions of metaphysical and spiritual truths, which use the language of imagination to communicate realities that transcend rational understanding.

Poetry, in its essence, shares with myth the ability to express the inexpressible and to reveal the invisible through symbolic and metaphorical language. Poetic language, instead of adhering to conceptual precision and linear logic, seeks to evoke emotions, awaken the imagination, and communicate profound truths through images, metaphors, rhythm, and sonority. The Aeons, in their transcendent and archetypal nature, find in poetry an ideal expressive medium for their manifestation. Aeonic poetry, present in hymns, invocations, and contemplative Neoplatonic and Gnostic texts, uses poetic language to describe the beauty, grandeur, and mystery of the Aeons, to express the devotion and aspiration of the soul towards these divine beings, and to evoke the experience of transcendence and mystical union. Poetry, in this context, becomes a vehicle for the contemplation and experience of the Aeons, opening the heart and mind to their transforming influence.

The presence of the Aeons in art, literature, and popular culture, both ancient and modern, attests to their appeal to human imagination and their capacity to inspire artistic creation. In ancient art, symbolic representations of celestial figures, concentric circles, mandalas, and other archetypal images can be interpreted as visual expressions of Aeonic reality, seeking to represent the Pleroma, the hierarchy of the Aeons, and the dynamics of divine emanation. In literature, themes such as the journey of the soul, the search for transcendence, the encounter with celestial beings, and the revelation of hidden truths, often present in mythical and epic narratives, can be seen as reflections of the influence of Aeonic thought, even if not explicitly named. In modern popular culture, in films, books, games, and other forms of artistic expression, Aeonic motifs and archetypes resurface in veiled or explicit ways, through characters that personify divine qualities, imaginary worlds that evoke hierarchized celestial realms, and narratives that explore the human search for meaning and transcendence. The presence of the Aeons in culture, in its diverse artistic manifestations, demonstrates their continuous resonance in the human imagination and their capacity to inspire creativity and symbolic expression.

Symbolic and metaphorical language, intrinsic to myth and poetry, becomes an essential instrument for understanding the Aeons, precisely because these beings transcend direct rational and conceptual apprehension. Symbolic language, instead of defining and delimiting, suggests and evokes, opening space for intuition, contemplation, and personal experience. Metaphors, allegories, archetypes, and poetic images, instead of describing the Aeons exhaustively and objectively, create bridges between the sensible world and the intelligible world, allowing the soul to glimpse, albeit indirectly and intuitively, the transcendent reality that the Aeons represent. Symbolic and metaphorical language is not limited to illustrating or ornamenting the concept of Aeons, but rather to revealing aspects of their nature that escape conceptual language, opening a portal to a deeper and more experiential understanding.

Imagination, in this context, is not understood as mere fantasy or arbitrary creation of the mind, but rather as a superior cognitive faculty, capable of intuiting truths that transcend discursive reason and of connecting with deeper and subtler levels of reality. Mythical and poetic imagination, when used consciously and intentionally, becomes a valid path of spiritual knowledge, a means for the soul to explore the realms of divine reality and to experience, even in a symbolic and imaginative way, the presence and influence of the Aeons. The practice of contemplating the Aeons through mythical and poetic imagination is not intended to replace reason or intellect, but rather to complement and transcend them, opening space for a more holistic and integrated understanding of divine reality, which involves not only the rational mind, but also emotion, intuition, and aesthetic sensibility.

It is important, however, to use mythical and poetic imagination in the contemplation of the Aeons with discernment and balance. Imagination, when uncontrolled or misdirected, can lead to misleading fantasies, subjective projections, and misinterpretations. The practice of contemplating the Aeons through imagination should always be anchored in a solid knowledge of Neoplatonic and Gnostic principles, and guided by intellectual intuition and spiritual wisdom, in order to avoid deviations and illusions. Mythical and poetic imagination, when used consciously and responsibly, becomes a powerful tool for spiritual exploration, opening paths to the understanding and experience of the Aeons, but it is essential to maintain a balance between imagination and discernment, between intuition and reason.

By allowing mythical and poetic imagination to flourish, the seeker not only enriches their understanding of the Aeons, but also rescues an ancestral form of wisdom, where knowledge intertwines with enchantment, and revelation arises in the interplay of living symbols and luminous images. In this symbolic tapestry, each metaphor becomes a portal, and each archetype a reflection of vaster realities, leading the soul to a territory where logical thought no longer reaches, but where intuitive perception recognizes, with familiarity, the pulsations of the divine. This immersion in the language of myth and poetry allows the mind itself to awaken to a contemplative state, where the invisible begins to whisper through forms, and beauty becomes a vehicle of truth.

In the dance between contemplation and creation, the seeker discovers that the soul itself is a mirror where the Aeons can be reflected. Each poetic image, each symbol imagined with devotion, functions as a call, a silent offering that invites these presences to inhabit the inner space. In this process, the soul not only contemplates the Aeons from a distance, but gradually becomes permeable to their influence, transforming contemplation into communion and enchantment into recognition. Through myth and poetry, the seeker recalls that spiritual truth is not always a sudden revelation or an intellectual certainty, but often a delicate thread of beauty and meaning that is revealed through enchantment and inner resonance.

Thus, mythical and poetic imagination, far from being a mere ornament or escape from reality, emerges as a legitimate path of access to the sacred, a forgotten language that speaks directly to the soul, awakening it from its sleep of literality. By allowing oneself to walk this path, the seeker learns to read symbols like one deciphers stars and to listen to the luminous silence between words. In this intermediate space, where form and essence intertwine, the Aeons cease to be mere metaphysical concepts and become living presences, internal guides that lead the soul not only to the contemplation of the divine, but to the discovery of the divine within itself.

Chapter 24
Archetypes of Human Experience

Throughout this journey through the Neoplatonic and Gnostic realms, the Aeons have emerged as luminous intermediary beings, personifications of divine qualities and steps on the ladder of spiritual ascension. However, the relevance of the Aeons is not limited to a distant cosmological system or an inaccessible celestial hierarchy.

Investigating the Aeons as archetypes reveals a more intimate and personal dimension of Neoplatonic knowledge, showing how metaphysical principles can connect with concrete human experience and how ancient wisdom can enrich our journey of self-discovery in the contemporary world. Perceiving the Aeons as archetypes transforms their contemplation into a powerful tool for self-knowledge and for the realization of human potential.

To understand the Aeons as archetypes, it is crucial to define the concept of archetype itself. In depth psychology, especially from a Jungian perspective, archetypes are understood as universal and primordial patterns of the human psyche, innate and collective psychic structures that manifest in recurring images, motifs, and experiences throughout history and in different cultures. Archetypes are not abstract ideas or intellectual concepts, but rather dynamic and living psychic forces that influence our thoughts, feelings, behaviors, and our perception of the world. They represent potentials and patterns of behavior inherent in the human psyche, manifesting symbolically and expressively in myths, dreams, art, and in the experience of life itself.

Within the Neoplatonic context, the Aeons, as personifications of divine qualities and emanations of the Intellect and the Soul, can be understood as primordial archetypes of divine reality and human experience. They are not only celestial beings external to us, but also internal archetypal images, present in the human psyche as potentials and patterns of consciousness and behavior. The universal and transcendent nature of the Aeons, their connection to fundamental divine qualities, and their role as mediators between the divine and the manifested world, make them ideal archetypes to represent essential dimensions of human experience, from the search for wisdom and love to the need for strength, justice, and beauty. When contemplating the Aeons, we are not only reflecting on distant celestial entities, but also coming into contact with internal archetypes, awakening dormant potentials in our own psyche, and recognizing universal patterns that shape our human experience.

The parallels between the qualities of the Aeons and the dimensions of the human psyche become evident when we examine the virtues personified by each Aeon and their resonance with our needs, desires, and capacities. The Aeon of Wisdom (Sophia), for example, manifests as the archetype of inner wisdom, of the enlightened intellect, of the pursuit of knowledge and profound understanding. In the human psyche, this archetype resonates with our innate thirst for meaning, for the search for answers to life's big questions, and for the development of our capacity for discernment and wisdom. The Aeon of Love (Agape), in turn, represents the archetype of unconditional love, of compassion, of union and connection with the other. In the human psyche, this archetype manifests in our deep desire to love and be loved, in the need for meaningful relationships, and in the capacity for empathy and compassion. The Aeon of Strength (Dynamis) personifies the archetype of inner strength, of will, of determination, and of the capacity to overcome. In the human psyche, this archetype resonates with our need for self-affirmation, for the achievement of goals, and with the ability to face challenges and persevere in the face of difficulties.

Other Aeons, such as that of Justice (Dikaiosyne), that of Beauty (Kallos), that of Peace (Eirene), and many others, also find resonance in archetypes of the human psyche, representing different dimensions of our experience and our values. The Aeon of Justice resonates with our innate sense of fairness and moral rectitude, the Aeon of Beauty with our aesthetic appreciation and the search for harmony, and the Aeon of Peace with our longing for inner tranquility and harmony with the world. By contemplating each Aeon and its specific divine quality, we can recognize and activate the corresponding archetypes in our own psyche, awakening dormant potentials and strengthening the virtues that elevate us and fulfill us as complete human beings.

The relevance of the Aeons as archetypes extends to the field of depth psychology and the journey of individuation. In the Jungian perspective, individuation is the process of integration and harmonization of the different archetypes of the psyche, aiming at the realization of the Self, the unifying center of the total personality. The Aeons, in this context, can be seen as archetypal models of individuation, representing the divine qualities that the human soul seeks to integrate and manifest in its journey of personal and spiritual growth. The ascension through the Aeonic hierarchy, described in previous chapters, can be interpreted as a metaphor for the journey of individuation, where each Aeonic step represents a stage of psychic development, a challenge to be overcome, and a virtue to be integrated.

The Aeons, in this archetypal reading, are not only external entities to be contemplated, but also internal forces to be recognized and integrated. The contemplation of the Aeons becomes a process of self-knowledge and inner transformation, where the soul recognizes itself in the divine archetypes, awakens to its own potentials, and opens itself to the transformative influence of divine qualities. In the journey of individuation, the Aeons can serve as guides and inspirations, offering models of perfection and fullness to be emulated, and indicating the paths for the integration of the shadow, the anima/animus, and the Self, the main archetypes of the Jungian psyche. By integrating the qualities of the Aeons, the soul becomes more complete, more harmonious, and more aligned with its divine purpose and potential.

Exploring the Aeons as archetypes of human experience thus becomes a powerful path to self-knowledge. By recognizing the archetypal patterns of the Aeons in our own psyche, we can gain profound insights into our motivations, desires, capacities, and challenges. Contemplation of the Aeon of Wisdom can reveal our thirst for knowledge and our particular way of seeking truth. Contemplation of the Aeon of Love can illuminate our capacity to love and our patterns of interpersonal relationships. Contemplation of the Aeon of Strength can reveal our will to power and our way of dealing with challenges and obstacles. The study of the Aeons as archetypes invites us to an intimate dialogue with our own psyche, to a recognition of the universal patterns that inhabit us, and to a journey of self-discovery and personal transformation.

By contemplating the Aeons as living archetypes within us, the boundary between the divine and the human begins to dissolve. Each virtue personified by the Aeons reveals itself as a latent seed in our soul, awaiting the moment to germinate and blossom into concrete experiences, daily choices, and intimate epiphanies. The Aeons cease to be merely cosmic steps in the grand scheme of universal emanation, becoming deep mirrors in which we recognize, in luminous and shaded reflections, the totality of who we are—our strengths, our vulnerabilities, and the vocation to become, ourselves, agents of divine manifestation in the world.

This archetypal perspective transforms the spiritual journey into a profoundly interior passage. By evoking each Aeon, we are not only opening ourselves to external celestial presences, but summoning hidden dimensions of our own psyche, awakening ancestral energies that shape our worldview, our relationships, and the way we face existence. This communion with the internal Aeons does not happen without tensions or challenges; each archetype carries with it the polarity of its lights and shadows, requiring discernment and courage from us to integrate, without denying or repressing, the contradictory forces that inhabit our essence.

In the end, perceiving the Aeons as archetypes of human experience is to recognize that cosmology and psychology, spirituality and self-knowledge, are not isolated domains, but complementary faces of the same process of return and remembrance. The Aeons, in their mythopoietic grandeur and in their intimate presence in the human heart, invite us to a radical reintegration: to be again children of light and wisdom, walkers between worlds, bearers of a cosmic heritage that is revealed to the extent that we dare to remember who we are and become co-creators of the reality we inhabit.

Chapter 25
Contemporary Spirituality

Following an exploratory journey through the foundations of Neoplatonism, the architecture of the primary hypostases, and the universe of Aeons as steps to the divine, we arrive at Part 4, dedicated to examining the Applications and Conclusions of this rich philosophical and spiritual system. We will explore the perennial nature of Neoplatonic questions, the relevance of its hierarchical and emanationist worldview, and its ability to dialogue with the various spiritual and philosophical currents of our time. The analysis of the contemporary relevance of Neoplatonism and hypostases aims to demonstrate that this tradition of thought, far from being merely a historical or academic interest, possesses a practical and transformative value for the spiritual and existential quest of modern human beings.

In the 21st century, characterized by a growing spiritual plurality and an individualized search for meaning and purpose, Neoplatonism re-emerges as a source of perennial and surprisingly current wisdom. In a world marked by secularization, moral relativism, and the fragmentation of knowledge, Neoplatonism offers a coherent and comprehensive worldview, capable of integrating reason, intuition, ethics, and mystical experience into a unified philosophical and spiritual system. Its emphasis on divine transcendence, the hierarchical cosmic order, the ascetic journey of the soul, and the quest for union with the supreme principle, resonates with the deep yearnings of contemporary human beings, who seek a deeper meaning for life, a connection with the transcendent, and a path to spiritual fulfillment.

The resonance of Neoplatonism and hypostases in the modern spiritual quest manifests in various areas and currents of thought. In the field of non-religious or secular spirituality, Neoplatonism offers a philosophical framework that allows exploring the spiritual dimension of human existence without resorting to religious dogmas or confessional institutions. Its emphasis on inner experience, contemplation, and self-transformation attracts those who seek a personal and authentic spiritual path, grounded in reason and direct experience, rather than adherence to pre-defined beliefs. The concept of hypostases, as progressively more subtle and transcendent levels of divine reality, offers a map for the exploration of consciousness and for the expansion of the perception of reality, compatible with a pluralistic worldview open to the diversity of spiritual experiences.

In the context of religious traditions, Neoplatonism continues to exert a remarkable influence, even if not always explicitly recognized. In Christianity, Neoplatonism profoundly influenced mystical theology, contemplative spirituality, and the understanding of divine nature, especially through the work of thinkers such as Pseudo-Dionysius the Areopagite, Meister Eckhart, and Saint John of the Cross. In Islam, Neoplatonism resonated with Sufi currents and Islamic philosophy, contributing to the elaboration of a metaphysics of the unity of being and a mystical path of union with the divine. In Judaism, Kabbalah and other mystical currents also present Neoplatonic elements, such as the idea of divine emanation, the hierarchy of spiritual worlds, and the quest for union with Ein Sof (the Infinite). The capacity of Neoplatonism to dialogue with and enrich various religious traditions demonstrates its perennial nature and its relevance for understanding religious experience in general.

The hierarchical and emanationist worldview of Neoplatonism, although sometimes criticized as outdated or incompatible with modern egalitarian thought, re-emerges with new force in the context of contemporary spirituality. In a world that experiences the increasing complexity of social, ecological, and informational systems, the idea of a hierarchical order, not as a rigid and oppressive structure, but as a dynamic and interdependent organization, becomes increasingly relevant for understanding reality. The hierarchy of hypostases, in this sense, can be reinterpreted as a model for thinking about the complexity and diversity of reality, recognizing the existence of different levels of organization, consciousness, and manifestation of being, without hierarchizing in a value-laden or exclusionary way. Emanation, as a process of progressive manifestation of reality from a primordial source, offers a powerful metaphor for understanding the interconnectedness of all things and the fundamental unity that underlies the diversity of the manifest world.

The Neoplatonic emphasis on contemplation and the ascetic journey also finds an echo in contemporary spirituality, in a context marked by the search for meditative and emotional self-regulation practices. Meditation techniques, mindfulness, and other contemplative practices, increasingly popular in the Western world, share with Neoplatonism the emphasis on interiorization, mental stillness, and the search for an expanded state of consciousness. The Neoplatonic ascetic journey, understood not as an escape from the world, but as a process of inner purification and cultivation of virtues, resonates with the contemporary search for authenticity, integrity, and personal development. The practice of contemplation and asceticism, in this sense, can be reinterpreted as a path to self-knowledge, to the reduction of suffering, and to the cultivation of qualities such as compassion, wisdom, and serenity, values increasingly valued in contemporary spirituality.

The concept of union with the divine, the ultimate goal of Neoplatonic philosophy, continues to inspire the modern spiritual quest, even in secular contexts. The experience of mystical union, described by Neoplatonists as a state of ecstasy, of transcendence of the ego, and of fusion with primordial reality, resonates with deep yearnings of the human soul, which seeks to overcome the limits of individuality and connect with something greater and more meaningful. The Neoplatonic language of mystical union, rich in metaphors and symbols, continues to inspire poets, artists, and spiritual seekers of all traditions, offering a vocabulary for describing transcendental experiences and altered states of consciousness. The quest for union with the divine, in this sense, can be reinterpreted as an innate yearning of the human soul for totality, integration, and transcendence, a fundamental impulse for the realization of human potential and for living a fuller and more meaningful life.

This resonance between Neoplatonism and contemporary spirituality does not occur by chance; it reveals a deep yearning of modern human beings for an integrated vision of existence, capable of uniting reason and intuition, science and mystery, interiority and cosmos. In a time where the fragmentation of experience is almost inevitable, Neoplatonic thought offers an axis of integration, where the visible and the invisible world, the personal and the transcendent, the immanent and the absolute intertwine in a continuous web of meaning. This reconnection with a hierarchical and sacred vision of reality can help the contemporary seeker rediscover a sense of cosmic belonging, where each life, each mind, and each soul has its place in the great circuit of being.

Furthermore, Neoplatonism provides the modern spirit with a proposal for self-knowledge that is not limited to the psychological dimension, but that expands the horizon of subjectivity to touch the margins of the divine. The inner journey is not reduced to an egoic self-reference, but is seen as a progressive ascent through the layers of one's own soul, until reaching the luminous principle from which everything emanates. This idea, that personal fulfillment is only achieved when inserted into the greater order of the cosmos, resonates deeply with those who, in the 21st century, intuit that the search for the meaning of life cannot be separated from the search for conscious participation in universal harmony.

Thus, Neoplatonism, emerging from antiquity to dialogue with the challenges of current spirituality, demonstrates that it is not merely an intellectual heritage, but a living wisdom that can enrich new syntheses and new practices of self-knowledge and spiritual connection. By reinterpreting the hypostases and the Aeons as interior maps, as psychic archetypes, and as metaphors for the very evolutionary process of consciousness, Neoplatonic thought reinvents itself without losing its essence. It reminds us, in times of ephemerality and information overload, that true knowledge is always a return—not only to the sources of thought, but to the luminous center of the soul, where the divine and the human meet as one.

Chapter 26
Personal Applications

After exploring the metaphysical architecture of Neoplatonism and the complex hierarchy of hypostases, it is natural to question ourselves about the practical relevance of this philosophical system to our daily lives. Far from being mere intellectual abstractions, hypostases and Neoplatonic principles offer a wealth of wisdom and tools to enrich our human experience, promote self-knowledge, and guide our spiritual journey in the concrete world.

Integrating hypostases into daily life is not about creating an escape from the world, but rather transforming our way of living and perceiving reality, infusing meaning, purpose, and a deep connection with the Divine into every moment of our existence.

One of the most direct ways to integrate the knowledge of hypostases into daily life is through contemplative reflection on the hierarchy of being. By understanding the emanationist structure of Neoplatonism, where reality flows from the transcendent One towards the manifest world, we can cultivate a deeper awareness of the interconnectedness of all things and our own place within the cosmic order. We can dedicate daily moments to contemplate the presence of the One as the primordial source of all existence, recognizing its transcendence and immanence in every aspect of reality. We can meditate on the Intellect (Nous) as the domain of divine thought, the seat of Platonic Forms, seeking to connect with the wisdom and cosmic intelligence that permeate the universe. We can reflect on the Soul (Psyché) as the animating and organizing principle of the cosmos, recognizing its vitalizing presence in ourselves, in other living beings, and in the nature that surrounds us. This exercise of contemplative reflection on the hypostases allows us to situate our personal experience within a broader cosmic context, infusing a sense of purpose and meaning into our existence and strengthening our connection with divine reality.

Another practical application of the knowledge of hypostases lies in the cultivation of virtue and Neoplatonic ethics. Neoplatonic philosophy, in describing the soul's journey towards the One as a process of purification and ascension, emphasizes the importance of the practice of virtue as an essential path to spiritual fulfillment. We can integrate Neoplatonic ethical principles into our daily lives, seeking to cultivate virtues such as wisdom, courage, justice, temperance, prudence, and faith. We can reflect on each of these virtues, understanding their Neoplatonic meaning and seeking to incorporate them into our thoughts, feelings, and actions. We can evaluate our daily conduct in the light of Neoplatonic ethical principles, identifying areas where we need improvement and seeking to align our behavior with the divine order. The cultivation of virtue, from this perspective, is not just a moral duty, but a transformative spiritual exercise that purifies the soul, draws it closer to the Divine, and contributes to the creation of a more harmonious and just world.

The practice of contemplation and meditation becomes a fundamental tool for integrating hypostases into daily life. We can dedicate regular moments for contemplative meditation, focusing our attention on each of the primary hypostases or on the Aeons, seeking to establish a deeper and more conscious connection with these levels of divine reality. We can use visualization techniques, imagining the radiant light of the One, the vastness of the Intellect, or the beauty of the World Soul. We can resort to mantras or inspiring phrases that help us concentrate the mind and attune our consciousness to the energy of the hypostases. We can practice mental stillness and inner silence, opening space for intuition and for the subtle perception of the divine presence in us and around us. Regular contemplative meditation strengthens our connection with the hypostases, calms the mind, expands consciousness, and promotes a state of peace and inner well-being that radiates into our daily lives.

Another practical way to integrate hypostases into daily life is through the application of Neoplatonic principles in interpersonal relationships. By understanding the interconnectedness of all souls and their common origin in the One, we can cultivate an attitude of compassion, empathy, and respect towards other human beings. We can seek to recognize the divine spark present in each person, regardless of their differences, imperfections, or beliefs. We can practice active listening, tolerance, and forgiveness, seeking to build more authentic, harmonious, and meaningful relationships. We can apply the principles of justice and equity in our social interactions, seeking to treat others with honesty, integrity, and consideration. The integration of Neoplatonic principles into interpersonal relationships transforms the way we interact with others, making us more compassionate, generous, and aware of our social responsibility and our interdependence as human beings.

The appreciation of beauty and harmony in nature and art also becomes a way to integrate hypostases into daily life. Neoplatonism, with its emphasis on beauty as an emanation of the Divine and as a path to contemplation, invites us to recognize the beauty that permeates the manifest world as a reflection of intelligible perfection. We can dedicate time to contemplate the beauty of nature, observing a sunrise, a flower garden, the sea, the mountains, or the starry sky, and recognizing in these natural manifestations the presence and energy of the World Soul and the Divine Intellect. We can appreciate the various forms of art, such as music, painting, sculpture, poetry, and dance, recognizing in them the expression of human creativity and the search for beauty and harmony. The contemplation of beauty and harmony in nature and art elevates our soul, expands our aesthetic sensibility, and strengthens our connection with the manifest Divine.

The search for the meaning of life and existential purpose can be enriched by understanding the hypostases. Neoplatonism, in describing the soul's journey as a return to the One, offers a map for the search for meaning and purpose in human existence. We can reflect on our own life purpose in the light of Neoplatonic principles, questioning ourselves about our place within the cosmic order, our mission, and how we can contribute to the manifestation of beauty, goodness, and truth in the world. We can seek to align our actions and choices with our deepest values, guided by Neoplatonic wisdom and the aspiration to union with the Divine. The understanding of hypostases, in this sense, not only offers a metaphysical framework for understanding reality, but also a practical guide for the search for a deeper and more meaningful purpose for our lives.

The integration of Neoplatonic thought into personal life, therefore, does not imply the adoption of a static or rigid view of spirituality, but rather the incorporation of a dynamic, open, and reflective posture towards existence. By recognizing that every moment of daily life can be permeated by the presence of the hypostases, we discover that spirituality is not restricted to isolated moments of meditation or contemplation, but overflows into small gestures, ethical choices, and the way we relate to the world and to others. This continuous awareness that we participate, albeit fragmentarily, in the harmony of the One, transforms the way we face challenges, how we welcome joys, and how we seek inner growth.

This vision, at once cosmic and intimate, invites us to balance the aspiration for transcendence with rootedness in the present. If each soul is a singular expression of the World Soul, each human experience carries within it the potential to reveal a spark of the divine, even in the most ordinary circumstances. In this way, Neoplatonic spiritual practice is not configured as an escape from sensible reality, but as an art of illuminating the concrete world with inner light, cultivating an awakened presence and a sensitivity capable of perceiving, in the ephemeral, echoes of the eternal.

In the end, the personal application of Neoplatonism reveals itself less as a set of prescriptions and more as an invitation to inner listening and constant attunement between the individual soul and cosmic harmony. It is in the creative tension between immanence and transcendence that the soul discovers its true dwelling place: a space of belonging that is, at the same time, path and destiny. In this journey, each act of virtue, each gesture of contemplation, each search for beauty and truth becomes not only an ethical or aesthetic affirmation, but a living bridge that reconnects the human to the divine and allows life, in its ordinary weave, to resonate with the song of eternity.

Chapter 27
The Meaning of Life

In the heart of the human experience lies a fundamental question, an unyielding yearning that echoes through the centuries: what is the meaning of life? Amidst the vastness of the cosmos and the ephemerality of individual existence, the search for meaning and purpose emerges as an inner compass, guiding our journey and shaping our choices. Neoplatonism, with its profound metaphysical architecture and its comprehensive vision of divine reality, offers a rich and structured answer to this perennial question, proposing a path to understanding the meaning of life intrinsically linked to the understanding of the hypostases and our relationship with the cosmic order.

The analysis of the Neoplatonic perspective on the meaning of life aims to offer a valuable counterpoint to contemporary currents of thought that sometimes emphasize the absurdity of existence or the absence of a transcendent purpose, revealing an alternative and profound path to understanding our place in the universe.

At the core of the Neoplatonic answer to the question of the meaning of life lies its emanationist and hierarchical cosmology. For Neoplatonism, reality is not a random set of events or a chaotic and purposeless universe, but rather an intrinsically meaningful cosmic order, which emanates from a primordial source of goodness and perfection: the One. Emanation itself, the process by which reality flows from the One towards multiplicity, is not a blind or accidental movement, but a necessary and teleological unfolding, driven by the overflowing nature of the One and its irradiation of good. Within this cosmology, human existence is not seen as a fortuitous accident or an unimportant byproduct, but as an integral and meaningful part of the cosmic order. Our own soul, as an emanation of the World Soul, participates in the cosmic dynamics and has a specific place within the hierarchy of being. This fundamentally meaningful cosmological framework already offers a first glimpse of an inherent meaning in life, detaching it from absurdity and inserting it into a context of divinely ordained order and purpose.

However, the meaning of life in Neoplatonism is not limited to occupying a predefined place within a cosmic hierarchy. The deepest purpose of human existence, in the Neoplatonic view, lies in the soul's journey towards returning to its primordial origin, the One. This "return," or *epistrophé*, as it is known in Neoplatonic vocabulary, is not merely a physical or spatial movement, but a spiritual and contemplative ascent, a process of purification and self-transcendence that leads the soul to recognize its essential identity with the Divine. Earthly life, with its challenges, sufferings, and joys, becomes, in this sense, a field of learning and purification, an opportunity for the soul to awaken from its illusion of separation and begin the path back to primordial unity. The meaning of life, therefore, is not something to be found in the external world, in material possessions or sensory pleasures, but something to be realized inwardly, through the ascetic journey of the soul towards the One. This transcendent purpose, the return to the divine source, gives human life a clear direction and a profound meaning, overcoming existential nihilism and offering a horizon of ultimate spiritual fulfillment.

Within this ascetic journey, the practice of virtue emerges as a crucial element for realizing the meaning of life. For Neoplatonism, virtue is not merely an external moral code or a set of social rules, but a set of inner qualities that align the soul with the divine order and facilitate its ascent. Cultivating virtues such as wisdom, justice, courage, and temperance is not just an ethical duty, but a transformative spiritual exercise that purifies the soul of its disordered passions, strengthens its will, and makes it more receptive to divine light. The virtuous life, therefore, is not only a path to personal morality or social harmony, but a path to the realization of the soul's purpose, to its progressive ascent and union with the Divine. The meaning of life, in this ethical perspective, is intrinsically linked to the practice of virtues and the pursuit of an existence aligned with the divine order, conferring upon moral action a transcendent meaning and a profound spiritual purpose.

Contemplation, especially the contemplation of the higher hypostases, such as the Intellect and the One, plays a central role in the Neoplatonic search for the meaning of life. Through contemplation, the soul transcends the sensible world and discursive thought, entering the domain of intellectual intuition and mystical experience. In the contemplation of the Intellect, the soul contacts the realm of Platonic Forms, the source of truth, beauty, and goodness, experiencing an expansion of consciousness and an intellectual illumination that reveal the intelligible nature of reality. In the contemplation of the One, the soul surpasses even the Intellect, transcending the subject-object duality and entering a state of mystical union, where its individuality dissolves into primordial and ineffable unity. These contemplative and mystical experiences not only offer a glimpse of divine reality, but also provide a direct experience of the meaning of life, an experience of fullness, beatitude, and connection with the source of all being and value. The meaning of life, therefore, can be found not only in the ascetic and ethical journey, but also in the contemplative and mystical experience, which offers a direct and transformative contact with divine reality and with the ultimate purpose of existence.

However, the meaning of life in Neoplatonism is not restricted to the transcendent search and mystical experience. Life in the manifest world, with its responsibilities and interactions, also has intrinsic meaning within the Neoplatonic vision. The manifestation of divine qualities in everyday life becomes an important way of realizing the meaning of life in the concrete world. By seeking to express virtues such as wisdom, love, justice, and beauty in our actions, relationships, and professional activities, we become instruments of the divine order in the manifest world, contributing to its harmony and manifestation. The meaning of life, in this practical perspective, is not found only in fleeing the world or in exclusively seeking transcendence, but also in the embodiment of divine qualities in earthly life, in the transformation of the world through virtuous action, and in the manifestation of divine light in every aspect of our existence.

In contrast to contemporary currents of thought that emphasize the absurdity of existence or the lack of transcendent meaning, Neoplatonism offers a worldview that intrinsically affirms the meaning and purpose of life. While existentialism, for example, sometimes highlights radical freedom and individual responsibility in the face of a universe without predefined meaning, Neoplatonism proposes that the meaning of life is inherent in the very structure of reality, inscribed in the cosmic order emanated from the Divine and realized in the ascetic journey of the soul towards its primordial source. Neoplatonism, unlike nihilism, does not deny the value of existence or the possibility of finding a transcendent purpose, but rather offers a clear and structured path to the discovery of the meaning of life, grounded in a profound metaphysics, a virtuous ethic, and a rich and transformative contemplative practice.

In this context, the meaning of life, far from being an insoluble mystery or an arbitrary construct, reveals itself as a call to reunite with our deepest nature, the one that pulsates at the center of the soul and echoes the harmony of the cosmos. The human trajectory, with its uncertainties and yearnings, is not seen as a blind wandering through absurd contingencies, but as a slow and patient reconnection with the primordial Source, a loving return to the One that, without haste, invites each soul to remember its origin. In this call, the soul discovers that meaning is not something that needs to be invented or imposed from the outside, but unveiled, like an ancestral melody that resonates in silence in the heart of existence.

The beauty of this vision lies precisely in its ability to reconcile transcendence and immanence, spirituality and daily life, mysticism and ethics. The meaning of life is not only in the contemplative culmination, in the rare moments of mystical fusion with the One, but also in daily care, in the bonds between souls, in the choices of each moment. Even the common experiences and adversities of earthly life become an integral part of this spiritual pilgrimage, as they are what offer the soul opportunities to exercise its virtues, to purify its passions, and to learn to see, behind the apparent multiplicity, the essential unity that sustains and nurtures all creation.

Thus, Neoplatonism not only offers a philosophical answer to the enigma of the meaning of life, but proposes a way of living where every gesture, every thought, and every encounter can be imbued with meaning. Each moment potentially becomes a door to the eternal; each act of love, a reflection of primordial unity; each sincere search for truth, a reverberation of cosmic intelligence. The meaning of life, therefore, is not a distant concept or an abstract idea, but a silent and compassionate presence that permeates the very fabric of existence — a presence that calls us, at every step, to awaken, remember, and return.

Chapter 28
Harmony with the Divine Order

Neoplatonic philosophy, in delineating the architecture of divine reality through hypostases, is not limited to an abstract metaphysical exercise, but also offers a solid foundation for a profound and comprehensive ethic. Understanding the divine order, the emanation from the One, and the hierarchy of being, not only illuminates our mind about the nature of reality, but also guides our conduct and shapes our character, leading us to a more virtuous and harmonious life, in consonance with cosmic principles. The analysis of Neoplatonic ethics reveals an ethical system intrinsically linked to metaphysics, where the pursuit of virtue and moral conduct are not merely human duties, but essential paths for the soul's ascension and union with the Divine.

The basis of Neoplatonic ethics lies in understanding the divine order and our position within that order. The Neoplatonic cosmos is not a chaotic or random universe, but a hierarchical order emanating from the One, where each being and each level of reality has a specific place and a particular function within the whole. Neoplatonic ethics, therefore, is not based on external rules or arbitrary commandments, but on the intrinsic nature of reality and our role as part of this order. To live ethically, from a Neoplatonic perspective, means to live in harmony with the divine order, recognizing our connection to the whole, understanding our specific function, and seeking to realize our potential according to our essential nature. Neoplatonic ethics is, thus, a cosmic ethic, which transcends individualistic or anthropocentric morality and is based on universal and objective principles, grounded in the structure of divine reality.

The fundamental ethical principle of Neoplatonism is the pursuit of virtue (areté). Virtue, in the Neoplatonic perspective, is not merely the absence of vice or the fulfillment of minimal moral rules, but the development of qualities that perfect the soul and bring it closer to the Divine. Neoplatonic virtues are intrinsically linked to the hypostases, manifesting as human expressions of the divine qualities that emanate from the One and radiate through the Intellect and the Soul. To cultivate virtue, therefore, means to become more like the Divine, participating in its perfection and beauty, and realizing our potential as rational and spiritual beings. Neoplatonic ethics is, thus, an ethic of perfection, which is not content with mediocrity or the minimally acceptable, but which aspires to excellence and the full realization of human potential, inspired by the model of divine perfection.

Among the Neoplatonic virtues, the cardinal virtues of the Platonic tradition stand out: wisdom (phronesis), justice (dikaiosyne), courage (andreia), and temperance (sophrosyne). Wisdom, for Neoplatonism, is the primordial virtue, the capacity to discern true good, to understand the order of reality, and to guide conduct by enlightened reason. Justice manifests as harmony and order, both in the individual soul and in society, seeking to give each one what is due and maintain balance in relationships. Courage is the inner strength to face challenges, overcome obstacles, and remain firm on the path of virtue, even in the face of adversity. Temperance represents the mastery of passions and desires, balance and moderation in all things, allowing reason to govern impulses and emotions. These cardinal virtues, together, form the foundation of the Neoplatonic ethical life, guiding the soul in the pursuit of perfection and inner and outer harmony.

Beyond the cardinal virtues, Neoplatonic ethics emphasizes other essential qualities, such as piety (eusebeia), faith (pistis), hope (elpis), and love (agape). Piety manifests as reverence and respect for the Divine, the recognition of its transcendence and our dependence on it, and the practice of prayer and contemplation as forms of spiritual connection. Faith is the confidence in divine goodness, in cosmic providence, and in the possibility of union with the One, even in the face of life's uncertainties and sufferings. Hope is the confident expectation of the realization of the ultimate good, the overcoming of evil, and eternal beatitude, keeping the soul oriented towards the transcendent future. Love, in its highest form (agape), represents union and harmony, universal benevolence, and the pursuit of the good of the other, reflecting the one and good nature of the Divine. These theological virtues, complementing the cardinal virtues, elevate Neoplatonic ethics beyond purely rational morality, infusing it with a spiritual and transcendent dimension.

In practice, living in harmony with the divine order, according to Neoplatonic ethics, implies a continuous process of self-examination, purification, and cultivation of virtues. Daily self-examination, vigilant moral conscience, and reflection on our actions and motivations become essential instruments for identifying our vices, our disordered passions, and our deviations from the path of virtue. Purification involves the constant effort to master passions, free oneself from material attachments and the illusions of the sensible world, and direct the soul towards higher and transcendent goods. The cultivation of virtues, finally, requires constant and deliberate practice, through meditation, contemplation, prayer, philosophical study, and virtuous action in the world. Neoplatonic ethics is not a set of easy rules to follow, but an arduous and demanding path of self-transformation, which requires continuous effort, discipline, and perseverance.

Neoplatonic ethics is not limited to the individual sphere, but also has social and political implications. Living in harmony with the divine order, from a Neoplatonic perspective, also implies seeking justice and harmony in human society. Social justice, understood as the equitable distribution of goods and opportunities, respect for the rights of others, and the promotion of the common good, becomes a reflection of cosmic justice and a fundamental ethical objective. Virtuous political action, inspired by Neoplatonic principles, seeks to promote the well-being of the community, govern with wisdom and justice, and create a society that is a reflection of divine order and harmony. Neoplatonic ethics, therefore, is not only an individualistic ethic, but also a social and political ethic, which recognizes the importance of community life and the pursuit of the common good as an integral part of the ethical and spiritual journey.

However, it is important to recognize the nuances and challenges of Neoplatonic ethics. Its emphasis on transcendence and the pursuit of divine perfection can sometimes result in a disdain for the sensible world and material needs, or in a detachment from concrete social and political concerns. Neoplatonic ethics, in its most radically ascetic form, can lead to a flight from the world and an exclusive pursuit of mystical union, neglecting the importance of action in the world and social transformation. It is essential, therefore, to interpret and apply Neoplatonic ethics in a balanced and integrated way, recognizing the importance of both the pursuit of transcendence and action in the world, both individual purification and social commitment, and seeking to manifest divine virtues in all dimensions of our existence.

Living in harmony with the divine order, in the Neoplatonic horizon, is more than obedience to a system of principles or the pursuit of irreproachable conduct; it is about tuning one's own soul to the silent music of the cosmos, allowing each choice, each thought, and each gesture to reverberate in tune with the ordering intelligence that sustains the universe. There is no separation between ethics and metaphysics, between behavior and contemplation, because virtuous action is not just an external manifestation, but a way of revealing, in the daily flow of existence, the inner light that points the way back to the One. Thus, harmony with the divine order is not just a goal, but a continuous process of realignment and inner listening, a delicate dance between the ascensional impulse of the soul and the concrete demands of incarnate life.

This path of harmony is not built in isolation or denial of the world, but in the discovery of the sacred amidst ordinary circumstances, in the perception that each encounter, each challenge, and each opportunity to exercise virtue are invitations to actualize, here and now, the intelligible perfection from which everything emanates. Social justice, care for others, the pursuit of beauty and truth become, in this context, not just ethical or aesthetic expressions, but modes of active participation in the cosmic order, mirroring in the sensible plane the intelligible harmony that animates all things. Each act of kindness, however simple, inscribes itself as an echo of primordial goodness, each gesture of wisdom resonates cosmic wisdom, and each reconciliation of opposites reflects the first unity where everything converges.

Ultimately, Neoplatonic ethics does not propose a rigid code, but an invitation to the soul's refinement, at once patient and ardent, towards the highest expression of what we already are in essence. To live in harmony with the divine order is to become a limpid mirror where the light of the One is reflected without distortions, allowing one's own existence to become a silent and continuous prayer. It is in this daily care, in this constant polishing, that the soul discovers that harmony is not an external imposition, but the loving remembrance of an ancestral melody, always present, just waiting to be heard again.

Chapter 29
Directions for Future Investigations

The journey through the pages of this book, dedicated to the exploration of Hypostases and Levels of Divine Reality in Neoplatonism, inevitably constitutes only a starting point for a vast and multifaceted field of study. Although we have traversed an extensive path, from the historical and philosophical foundations to the practical applications and ethical implications of this tradition of thought, it is essential to recognize that Neoplatonism, in its depth and complexity, continues to raise open questions and demand future investigations.

In outlining these areas of future investigation, we seek not only to acknowledge the limits of our own study but also to encourage the continuation of exploration and the deepening of knowledge about this philosophical and spiritual system of perennial relevance.

One of the most evident areas of open questions lies in the very interpretation and precise definition of Neoplatonic concepts, especially concerning the nature of the Hypostases and the Aeons. Despite the extensive body of primary texts and the vast secondary literature dedicated to the topic, ambiguities and interpretative nuances persist in relation to fundamental concepts such as the nature of the One, the precise distinction between the primary Hypostases, the hierarchy and functions of the Aeons, and the dynamics of emanation and conversion. Future investigations may delve deeper into the meticulous textual analysis of the works of Plotinus, Porphyry, Iamblichus, Proclus, and other Neoplatonists, seeking to clarify terminological ambiguities, unravel different interpretative perspectives, and reconstruct in a more precise and nuanced way the metaphysical architecture of Neoplatonism. The use of tools from analytical philosophy and contemporary textual criticism can contribute to refining our understanding of Neoplatonic concepts and to overcoming some of the interpretative difficulties that persist.

Another promising direction for future investigations lies in the historical and cultural contextualization of Neoplatonism. Although we have addressed the general historical context of Neoplatonism at the beginning of this book, many questions remain open about the precise influences that shaped Neoplatonic thought and about its impact on the late Hellenistic world and late Antiquity. Future research may explore in more depth the relations of Neoplatonism with other philosophical and religious currents of the time, such as Gnosticism, Hermetism, nascent Christianity, and the mystery religions. Investigations into the social, political, and cultural context of Neoplatonism may reveal how Neoplatonic ideas developed and spread in different urban centers, such as Alexandria, Rome, and Athens, and how they interacted with the social and political dynamics of the time. The analysis of historical and archaeological sources, complementing the reading of philosophical texts, can enrich our understanding of Neoplatonism as a complex and multifaceted cultural phenomenon.

Comparative approaches represent another fertile avenue for future investigations into Neoplatonism and the hypostases. Although we have sketched some comparisons between Neoplatonism and other spiritual traditions throughout this book, there is a vast field to be explored in the systematic comparison of Neoplatonism with other mystical and philosophical currents, both Western and Eastern. Future research may investigate the parallels and differences between Neoplatonic cosmology and the cosmologies of other traditions, such as Hinduism, Buddhism, Taoism, Kabbalah, Sufism, and Christian Mysticism, seeking to identify universal themes of mystical experience and spiritual seeking that transcend the particularities of each tradition. The comparison between Neoplatonism and modern Western philosophy, especially with currents such as German Idealism, Existentialism, and Phenomenology, can also reveal points of contact and enriching dialogues, demonstrating the perenniality and relevance of Neoplatonic thought for contemporary philosophy.

The contemporary relevance of Neoplatonism and the hypostases is another area that demands future investigations and approfondissements. Although we have explored some applications of Neoplatonism in contemporary spirituality and daily life, there is a vast field to be explored regarding the practical and theoretical applications of Neoplatonism in the 21st century. Future research may investigate the relevance of Neoplatonism to contemporary issues such as environmental ethics, social justice, depth psychology, consciousness, artificial intelligence, and the search for meaning and purpose in the secular age. The application of Neoplatonic principles in different areas of knowledge and human practice may reveal new perspectives and solutions for the challenges of the contemporary world, demonstrating the vitality and topicality of this ancestral wisdom.

A more specific focus on less studied Neoplatonists and less explored texts also represents a valuable direction for future investigations. Although Plotinus, Porphyry, Iamblichus, and Proclus have received considerable academic attention, there are other important Neoplatonists, such as Syrianus, Damascius, Olympiodorus, and Simplicius, whose works deserve greater exploration and analysis. The translation and study of lesser-known Neoplatonic texts can reveal new nuances and perspectives on the Hypostases and the Aeons, enriching our understanding of Neoplatonism as a whole. Comparative analysis between different Neoplatonists, focusing on their interpretative divergences and convergences, can also contribute to a more complete and nuanced view of the evolution of Neoplatonic thought throughout late Antiquity.

Finally, the methodological approaches used in the study of Neoplatonism can be enriched and diversified. In addition to traditional philosophical and historical approaches, future investigations may benefit from the incorporation of methodologies from other areas of knowledge, such as phenomenology, hermeneutics, critical theory, gender studies, and cultural studies. The use of digital tools and computational text analysis can also open new perspectives for the investigation of the Neoplatonic corpus, allowing for the quantitative analysis of vocabulary, concepts, and intertextualities. The diversification of methodological approaches can enrich the academic debate and open new paths for the understanding of Neoplatonism and the hypostases in the 21st century.

In this horizon of possibilities, Neoplatonism reveals itself not only as an object of philosophical or historical study but as a living tradition, capable of dialoguing with the most pressing concerns of today. Each new investigation, by revisiting its sources and unfolding its implications, not only deepens the understanding of the tradition itself but contributes to reactivating its transformative potential, shedding light on questions of identity, transcendence, and meaning that continue to pulsate in the heart of human experience. The future of Neoplatonic research, therefore, is not an exercise in erudition detached from life but a constant invitation to re-examine how we understand ourselves, the world, and the mysterious Presence that permeates the totality of the real.

Furthermore, the broadening of comparative and intercultural approaches will allow Neoplatonism to be recognized not only as a singular expression of late Hellenistic philosophy but as a particular instance of a universal longing: the search for the order hidden beneath apparent chaos, for the unity underlying diversity, for the silent center that sustains the infinite dance of forms. Connecting these Neoplatonic intuitions with spiritual, scientific, and philosophical traditions of other times and cultures enriches not only the understanding of Neoplatonism but also the possibility of elaborating a more integrated and comprehensive view of the human condition itself.

With this, this journey, even if finished in its pages, remains open in its purpose. Each future investigation, each renewed reflection on the hypostases and the divine order, expands not only the academic field but the very interior space of each seeker, philosopher, or contemplative. Just as the soul, which never ceases to return to the One, the study of Neoplatonism does not end but curves upon itself in a perpetual movement of return and rediscovery — an invitation to continue thinking, living, and listening, always in search of that subtle harmony that reverberates between the visible and the invisible.

Chapter 30
Towards the Divine

As we reach the end of this in-depth exploration of the Hypostases and Levels of Divine Reality in Neoplatonism, it is crucial to reflect on the intrinsic importance of this study and its lasting value beyond the historical and philosophical context. Neoplatonism, with its complex metaphysical architecture and its profound spiritual vision, is not merely an ancient system of thought to be academically dissected, but rather a perennial source of wisdom and guidance for the human soul in its search for meaning, purpose, and connection with the transcendent. Dedicating time and effort to the study of the hypostases and Neoplatonism transcends the mere acquisition of intellectual knowledge; it is an investment in our own journey of self-knowledge and spiritual growth, a dive into the depths of being that resonate with universal and timeless yearnings.

The study of the hypostases, in particular, offers us a detailed and sophisticated map of divine reality, a conceptual framework that allows us to organize and understand the vastness and complexity of the spiritual realm. Instead of a simplistic and linear view of the divine, Neoplatonism presents us with a hierarchy of levels of reality, each emanating from the previous one and participating in the perfection of the One, while maintaining its own distinction and function. This hierarchical understanding does not imply a hierarchical valuation in the pejorative sense, but rather the recognition of the diversity and richness of divine manifestation, from the ineffable unity of the One to the multiplicity of the sensible world. This conceptual map offers us a language to describe and navigate the different dimensions of spiritual experience, from states of intellectual contemplation to moments of mystical union, allowing us to understand our own spiritual journey within a broader and more coherent context.

Beyond the mapping of divine reality, Neoplatonism, in its totality, offers us a practical path for inner transformation and spiritual realization. The emphasis on the practice of virtue, contemplation, and asceticism is not limited to a set of moral precepts or isolated meditative techniques, but rather configures an integrated system of life, where the pursuit of moral excellence, the cultivation of the contemplative mind, and the effort of inner purification are intertwined in an ascending path towards the Divine. The study of Neoplatonism invites us to question our values, to examine our habits, and to reorient our lives towards higher principles, inspired by divine wisdom and beauty. This invitation to personal transformation, this appeal to the pursuit of inner perfection, is perhaps one of Neoplatonism's most valuable contributions to contemporary spirituality, offering an antidote to the nihilism, materialism, and superficiality that sometimes characterize modern culture.

Reiteration of the book's main message: the search for union with the divine is a continuous journey.

Throughout all chapters, a central message has resonated like a guiding thread, permeating the complexity of Neoplatonic metaphysics and the diversity of its spiritual practices: the search for union with the Divine is a continuous journey, a process that extends throughout life and that transcends the search for definitive answers or simplistic solutions. Neoplatonism does not offer a final destination to be reached in a single step, nor an infallible instruction manual for instant enlightenment, but rather a map for a long and challenging journey, where each step, each conquest, and each obstacle overcome contribute to the progressive approximation of the soul to its divine source.

This message of the continuous journey is fundamental for understanding the essence of Neoplatonic spirituality and for avoiding reductive or mistaken interpretations. Union with the Divine is not understood as a static or definitive state to be achieved once and for all, but rather as a dynamic and constantly evolving process, a dance between the soul and the Divine that unfolds over time and eternity. Even in moments of mystical ecstasy or deep contemplation, the soul does not fix itself in an immutable state of union, but rather experiences a glimpse of divine reality that impels it to continue the journey, to deepen its search, and to expand its consciousness. Earthly life, with its limitations and challenges, becomes, in this perspective, not an obstacle to be overcome or a prison to be freed from, but rather the very field of realization of the spiritual journey, the space where the soul purifies itself, develops, and draws ever closer to the Divine, in every moment, in every experience, in every encounter.

Encouragement to the reader to deepen their knowledge and personal experience with Neoplatonism.

We have reached the end of this work, but the journey of exploring Neoplatonism and the hypostases is far from over. On the contrary, this book aims to be an invitation for the reader to deepen their own knowledge and personal experience with this rich tradition of thought. The preceding pages have offered only an introduction, an initial map to a vast and multifaceted territory, and there is much more to be discovered, explored, and experienced. Neoplatonism, in its essence, is a living philosophy, which is nourished by personal reflection, contemplative experience, and the sincere search for truth and goodness.

I encourage the reader to continue reading the original texts of the Neoplatonists, to immerse themselves in the wisdom of Plotinus, Porphyry, Iamblichus, Proclus, and other masters of this tradition, allowing themselves to be guided by their rich and evocative language and the depth of their insights. I invite you to explore the vast secondary literature dedicated to Neoplatonism, to delve into academic debates and different interpretations, and to form your own understanding of this system of thought, in a critical and reflective way. I encourage you to experiment with Neoplatonic contemplative practices, to dedicate time to meditation, prayer, silent reflection, and the search for altered states of consciousness, seeking to experience for yourself the divine reality that Neoplatonism describes. And, above all, I exhort you to integrate Neoplatonic principles into your daily life, to seek to live in a more virtuous, more conscious, and more aligned way with the divine order, manifesting the light and goodness of the Divine in every aspect of your existence.

Thus, Neoplatonism remains a living bridge between the finite and the infinite, between what we are and what we aspire to be. More than a philosophical system enclosed in treatises and commentaries, it reveals itself as a silent convocation—a call for each soul to remember its origin and, in remembering it, rediscover its true path. Each reflection, each contemplative practice, each gesture inspired by this vision of the divine order is a step in this return, an affirmation that, even amidst the shadows and dispersions of daily life, the One never ceases to draw us back to its silent fullness.

By treading this path, the seeker not only discovers metaphysical truths but discovers himself in a deeper and more essential dimension. The Neoplatonic journey is, ultimately, a vertical voyage, a progressive ascent where knowledge and inner experience are intertwined, purifying the senses, ordering desires, and expanding the mind until personal identity itself unfolds in the transparency of the One. Each reading, each contemplation, and each act of virtue thus become small portals, opening the soul to a reality that, even transcending it, pulsates silently within it.

The true invitation of this book, therefore, is for the reader not to remain only on the conceptual or historical plane, but to take this search for themselves, inscribing it into the rhythm of their own life. May the hypostases not be merely descriptions of a distant cosmos, but living layers of their own soul, echoes of an inner harmony waiting to be awakened. For, as the Neoplatonists always knew, to understand is already to begin to return—and to return is to discover, in each step, that the light we seek outside is the same that burns in silence within us.

Epilogue

Every journey of genuine knowledge does not end with the last page of a book. It begins a new cycle, an unfolding of consciousness that can never be reversed. If you have come this far, something within you has been touched, even if subtly. Neoplatonism is not a philosophy to be merely studied – it is a way of seeing and living in the world.

Throughout these pages, you have been led to a broader perception of reality: a universe structured in levels of existence, interconnected by a cosmic order invisible to the eyes, but perceptible to the soul. The One, Intellect, and Soul are no longer just philosophical concepts, but keys that unlock a deeper understanding of the very essence of life. The Aeons and Archangels have ceased to be mythological figures and have become living forces, intermediaries between our limited consciousness and the emanations of the sacred.

But the fundamental question remains: what to do with this knowledge?

The call that echoes in Neoplatonism is not an invitation to mere contemplation, but to integration. With every thought that emerges, with every reflection, there is the possibility of aligning oneself with the divine order and becoming an agent of that harmony in the sensible world. The ascent of the soul does not occur only in mystical states or deep meditations – it manifests itself in everyday life, in the way we look at others, at ourselves, and at the universe itself.

Now, the choice is yours. You can close this book and allow the ideas contained within it to dissipate in the flow of time. Or you can carry this knowledge with you, like a beacon that illuminates the search for the return to the primordial source.

Glossary of Neoplatonic Terms

Neoplatonic vocabulary, rich in nuances and derived from ancient Greek, can sometimes present challenges for those approaching this system of thought for the first time. This glossary aims to demystify Neoplatonic language, providing concise and accessible definitions of the most important terms, and allowing the reader to navigate the conceptual universe of Neoplatonism with greater confidence and understanding. Consulting this glossary may assist in reading and rereading the preceding chapters, reinforcing the apprehension of key concepts and consolidating the knowledge acquired throughout this exploration. This glossary is not intended to be exhaustive, but rather functional and practical, focusing on the terms most relevant to the understanding of the Hypostases and Levels of Divine Reality in Neoplatonism.

Aeon (Aion): Greek term meaning "era," "age," or "eternity." In the Neoplatonic and Gnostic context, Aeons are intermediary beings, emanations of the Divinity, who inhabit the Pleroma and personify divine qualities. They are often organized into complex hierarchies and act as mediators between the transcendent Divine and the manifested world.

Agape: Greek term designating unconditional, altruistic, and spiritual love. In Neoplatonism, Agape is seen as an essential divine quality, a unifying force that emanates from the One and manifests at different levels of reality. It is the love that aspires to good, beauty, and truth, and that seeks union with the Divine.

Analogy: Fundamental philosophical reasoning method in Neoplatonism. Analogy allows establishing correspondences and relationships of similarity between different levels of reality, from the sensible world to the intelligible world and the transcendent Divine. Through analogy, it is possible to understand the unknowable through the knowable, using the experiences of the manifested world as symbols and reflections of divine reality.

Anima Mundi (World Soul): Neoplatonic concept designating the cosmic Soul, the animating and organizing principle of the sensible universe. The World Soul is an emanation of the Soul Hypostasis and acts as a mediator between the intelligible world and the material world, conferring life, order, and beauty to the cosmos.

Archetype: Universal and primordial pattern of the human psyche, according to Jungian psychology. In the Neoplatonic context, Aeons can be interpreted as archetypes of human experience, personifying divine qualities and reflecting deep dimensions of the psyche.

Ascension (Anagogé): Journey of the soul towards the Divine in Neoplatonism. Ascension is a gradual process of purification, contemplation, and mystical union, which leads the soul to transcend the sensible world, ascend through the hypostases, and return to its primordial origin, the One.

Contemplation (Theoria): Central practice in Neoplatonic philosophy, which consists of focused and silent attention on intelligible and divine reality. Contemplation aims to transcend discursive thought and sensory perception, allowing the soul to directly intuit truth, beauty, and good, and to achieve mystical union with the Divine.

Demiurge: Figure present in Plato's philosophy and reinterpreted in Neoplatonism. The Demiurge is the divine craftsman, the ordering and creating principle of the sensible universe, who models chaotic matter according to the intelligible Platonic Forms. In the Neoplatonic system, the Demiurge is often associated with the Intellect or the Soul.

Dianoia: Greek term referring to discursive thought, logical reason, and the process of sequential reasoning. In Neoplatonism, Dianoia is seen as a faculty inferior to Nous (Intellect), which operates at the level of the rational soul and deals with the sensible and intelligible world, but indirectly and mediatedly.

Emanation (Próodos): Fundamental process in Neoplatonic cosmology, through which reality flows from the One to multiplicity. Emanation is a necessary and spontaneous unfolding of the overflowing nature of the One, an irradiation of being, intelligence, and life that manifests at different levels of reality, the Hypostases.

Epistrophe (Conversion/Return): Movement of return of the soul to its divine origin in Neoplatonism.

Epistrophe complements Proodos (Emanation), describing the ascetic journey of the soul, its effort to purify itself, contemplate the Divine, and achieve mystical union with the One.

Ecstasy (Ekstasis): State of mystical transcendence in Neoplatonism, characterized by the soul's departure from itself and its immediate and ineffable union with the Divine. Ecstasy represents the ultimate goal of the Neoplatonic ascetic journey, the experience of divine fullness and beatitude.

Hypostasis (Hypóstasis): Greek term meaning "substrate," "underlying reality," or "substantial existence." In Neoplatonism, Hypostases are the levels of divine reality, hierarchically ordered and emanated from the One. The main Hypostases are the One, the Intellect, and the Soul.

Intellect (Nous): Second Hypostasis in the Neoplatonic system, emanation of the One and domain of divine thought. The Intellect is the realm of Platonic Forms, of intelligible truth, beauty, and good. It is the first manifestation of multiplicity from the unity of the One and the source of intelligence and order in the cosmos.

Logos: Greek term with multiple meanings, including "word," "reason," "principle," or "order." In Neoplatonism, the Logos is often associated with the Intellect and its ordering and manifesting function of divine intelligence in the cosmos.

Hen (The One): First Hypostasis and supreme principle of Neoplatonism. The One is transcendent, ineffable, and unknowable, primordial source of all reality, goodness, and beauty. It is absolute unity, beyond being and non-being, the origin and the end of all emanation.

Noesis: Greek term referring to intellectual intuition, the immediate and non-discursive apprehension of truth. In Neoplatonism, Noesis is the superior faculty of the soul, which allows direct contact with intelligible and divine reality, especially with the Intellect and the Platonic Forms.

Pleroma: Greek term meaning "fullness." In the Gnostic and Neoplatonic context, the Pleroma designates the realm of Divine Fullness, inhabited by the Aeons and manifestation of the richness and diversity of the Divinity.

Psyché (Soul): Third Hypostasis in the Neoplatonic system, emanation of the Intellect and animating principle of the cosmos. Psyché is a mediator between the intelligible world and the sensible world, conferring life, movement, and order to material reality. It includes the World Soul and individual souls.

Theurgy: Ritualistic and ceremonial practices in late Neoplatonism, which aimed to establish communication and union with gods and other spiritual entities, seeking purification, illumination, and divine aid.

Transcendence: Fundamental characteristic of the Divine in Neoplatonism, referring to its nature that surpasses and exceeds the sensible world and human thought. The One is transcendent to all manifested reality, ineffable and unknowable by discursive reason.

Virtue (Areté): Moral and spiritual quality that perfects the soul and brings it closer to the Divine in Neoplatonism. Neoplatonic virtues include the cardinal virtues (wisdom, justice, courage, temperance) and the theological virtues (piety, faith, hope, love). The practice of virtue is essential for the ascetic journey of the soul.

This glossary, far from being exhaustive, seeks to offer a useful reference point for the reader who ventures into the study of Neoplatonism. Familiarity with these key terms will facilitate the understanding of the concepts and ideas presented throughout this book, and may serve as a springboard for future explorations and deepenings in the vast and fascinating universe of Neoplatonic thought.

www.ingramcontent.com/pod-product-compliance
Lightning Source LLC
LaVergne TN
LVHW040054080526
838202LV00045B/3628